EXIT LAUGHING

Also by Victoria Zackheim

Fiction

The Bone Weaver

Anthologies

*The Other Woman: Twenty-one Wives, Lovers, and Others Talk
Openly about Sex, Deception, Love, and Betrayal*

*For Keeps: Women Tell the Truth about Their Bodies,
Growing Older, and Acceptance*

*The Face in the Mirror: Writers Reflect on Their Dreams
of Youth and the Reality of Age*

*He Said What? Women Write about Moments
When Everything Changed*

Theater

A Deadly Competition

The Other Woman

Documentary Films

*Where Birds Never Sang: The Story of Ravensbrück
and Sachsenhausen Concentration Camps*

Tracing Thalidomide: The Frances Kelsey Story

Feature Films

Maidstone

EXIT LAUGHING

How Humor
Takes the Sting Out of Death

Edited by
VICTORIA ZACKHEIM

North Atlantic Books
Berkeley, California

Published by
North Atlantic Books
P.O. Box 12327
Berkeley, California 94712

Cover and book design by Brad Greene
Printed in the United States of America

This is issue #71 in the Io series.

Exit Laughing: How Humor Takes the Sting Out of Death is sponsored by the Society for the Study of Native Arts and Sciences, a nonprofit educational corporation whose goals are to develop an educational and cross-cultural perspective linking various scientific, social, and artistic fields; to nurture a holistic view of arts, sciences, humanities, and healing; and to publish and distribute literature on the relationship of mind, body, and nature.

North Atlantic Books' publications are available through most bookstores. For further information, visit our website at www.northatlanticbooks.com or call 800-733-3000.

Library of Congress Cataloging-in-Publication Data

Exit laughing : how humor takes the sting out of death / edited by Victoria Zackheim.
    p. cm.
  Summary: "In *Exit Laughing*, author and editor Victoria Zackheim, along with twenty-three other contributing writers, examines the humorous side of our mortality"—Provided by publisher.
  ISBN 978-1-58394-407-3 (pbk.)
  1. Death—Humor. I. Zackheim, Victoria.
  PN6231.D35E95 2012
  818'.602—dc23

                                                    2011042095

1 2 3 4 5 6 7 8 9 UNITED 17 16 15 14 13 12
Printed on recycled paper

In memory of GG

CONTENTS

INTRODUCTION

There's nothing funny about dying. Or is there?

My mother, who had been fiercely independent and active for the first eighty-seven years of her life, fell ill in 2009 and became fragile. There were months at a time when I was with her from early morning until her bedtime, and spent considerable time urging her to eat, take her meds, and go for a little walk. When I pushed, she accused me of acting more like a nursing supervisor than an attentive daughter. I recall her being annoyed by something I'd done (or said, thought, worn, eaten, who remembers?) and I gave her one of *those* looks. She told me, "You'll miss me when I'm dead," and I replied, "Die first, and then I'll know." Despite our complicated relationship—or perhaps because of it—we laughed and moved on to another subject, relieved not to have fallen into one of those deep conversations that neither of us wanted to have.

When we realized that she was dying, we fell back into that shared humor because we discovered that it opened doors to subjects we had wanted to discuss, but had never found the right moment. Humor, we learned, creates those moments.

Studies have long shown that people who laugh have a more positive outlook on life. But what about people who know that they are dying? Do they manage their pain, prolong their lives, or make the quality of their lives better through humor? And those friends and family members close to someone who is dying—how do they relate when death is near?

As I spent more time with my mother, something changed in the way we communicated. I'm convinced that it wasn't because of her memory loss or difficulty focusing, rather an awareness that her life would never return to normal. Had I thought about it, I might have foreseen this change, but I was focused on meeting deadlines, as well as seeing to her next dosage of medicine, or making sure she was clean, fed, dignified, and wearing her dentures so visitors would not face a toothless woman. While our conversations continued regarding her state of health—with most of my questions and comments eliciting the expected, "Oh, Vicki, please stop!"—they often segued into moments of unbridled laughter.

I've always known how important humor was to my mother—and yes, we shared a love of rather dark humor—but her life was coming to an end . . . how funny could that be?

I often wonder what it is about death that our society cannot confront. Is it the finality? The unknown? And with all this confusion and avoidance we wrap around dying, is it so surprising that we are sometimes forced to use humor to ease us through? We are a people ill at ease with not only the discussion but the entire process of dying, death, and grieving. In those long visits with my mother, I learned that there are emotions other than terror, sadness, and regret that serve to accompany us on this journey. One can share the pleasure of a life well lived, the joy of having taken journeys to faraway places, the bliss of holding a great-grandchild—all that we have achieved, rather than what we will miss.

I've never felt inept when it comes to talking about death.

A dear friend in Holland shared with me just weeks before dying that I was her only friend willing and available to discuss her death. She was desperate to talk about it—an unmarried woman leaving behind a young daughter—but her friends and family insisted that she would rally, that the widely metastasized cancer would magically disappear. She needed a receptive ear so she could talk through her concerns and sort out her daughter's future. Our friendship was one of my greatest gifts, and it meant so much to me, even long after her death, that I could give this to her.

It was with trepidation and some discomfort that my mother and I began to explore many of the issues related to the realities of her death. How limited was her time? (More limited than I believed.) What happens after death? (As an atheist, that answer was no challenge to her.) Was there time to resolve conflicts she had created with some of her grandchildren? What had her life meant to her family, to her friends, and to her, and what would it mean after she was gone?

Within weeks of my mother's death, I began to explore even further how so many of us use humor to ease pain and the important role humor can play in helping us confront the one issue that seems to trouble so many of us and elude our ability to understand it: that is, how to talk about and accept the death of someone we love. In the time since my mother's death, I have found myself going back again and again to those moments of closeness, of humor, and finding solace as I replay the conversations—and the laughs—we shared.

Some believe that death marks the beginning of another life, while others hold that death is the end, with nothing awaiting us. Whatever our beliefs, we hope that in some way they comfort us as we approach death and that we can accept the end without fear. For me, acceptance of death comes from a continuum that begins with living a life well lived. I hope that the end stages of my life are lived without fear and with plenty of humor.

I'm not saying that humor is the elixir to soothe our pain—but I do believe it can open a door to emotions shared, and perhaps through this sharing we can not only process the reality of death but mend the complex and often difficult relationships we share with the person who is dying. Humor is also a way that we mock death, ward it off in the hope (conscious or not) that it will pass over our houses and leave us be.

From those months spent with my dying mother and from my own thoughts and musings that followed come this collection of personal essays written by some of our country's most prominent authors, twenty-four men and women sharing their experiences around humor and death. From four leading citizens trapped in a mental hospital after a friend's wake (with all identification locked safely in the car, how could they convince security to release them?), to a husband commiserating over the death of a grandmother (when it was actually the cat who died); from siblings standing at their father's casket attempting to suppress relief that this brutal man was finally dead, to the hearse driver who gets lost and leads a caravan of mourners into neighborhoods of unsuspecting families, the stories are poignant, very personal, sometimes hilarious, and always factual. Each one reminds us in some way that, despite living in a society obsessed with communication, death is so often presented as something not to be discussed. (As Malachy McCourt points out in "Another Expiration Date," we have more euphemisms for *dead* than perhaps any society on earth.)

Whether you are reading playful banter or exploring the pain of loss, *Exit Laughing* provides insights into each author's warm, often biting, and always compelling wit. As we explore the subject of humor, you will recognize how often it becomes not only a release from tension and pain but a way of coming to terms with death itself.

Perhaps this book will offer comfort and peace in the face of one of life's most difficult times, helpful for those experiencing the grieving process. Even more important, it is my wish that this book, laughs and all, opens the window into our hearts.

—Victoria Zackheim
San Francisco, 2012

ANOTHER EXPIRATION DATE

— Malachy McCourt —

One of the reasons I left Ireland was that, whilst death is not always fatal there, people do die, unlike in the USA, where there seem to be some other arrangements for dying. Here is a partial list of what happens to people in a country where uncontrolled euphemisms trample news of death to death: she is deceased, gone now, laid to rest, at peace, now in heaven; he became an angel, joined the heavenly choir, found tranquility, entered the Garden of Eden, left us suddenly; she has joined her husband in eternal life, went home to be with the Lord, is in a better place; he breathed his last, is beneath the sod, is in his final sleep, has gone to his eternal reward, is wandering the Elysian Fields, said his last goodbye, entered the great void, laid down his knife and fork, took his last curtain call, entered the pearly gates, met his demise; she reached her final destination, encountered the Grim Reaper, departed this life, expired, is in God's arms; we suffered bereavement, we said goodbye to Grandpa; he made his final exit, stepped off to eternity, is no longer with us, met his end, left this life for another; she is history, pushing up the daisies; he is planted, bit the dust, kicked the bucket, bought the farm, succumbed, crossed the River Styx, bought a pine condo, sprouted wings, danced his last dance, shuffled off this mortal coil, cashed in his chips, is no longer with us; and the most common of all: he passed. The question being, What? And who is going to clean up? And death is forbidden in public places; as the signs on various highways proclaim, "No Passing."

I can say with certitude that the longer you live, the more people you know will die, which is like saying that when people are out of work it's because of unemployment. And, generally speaking, it seems to be quite in order for our parents to die before us, as obviously mine did, and here's a bit of my mother's dying saga. (A note here: the title of my brother's book, *Angela's Ashes*, arose from her heavy smoking and the fact that she ended up being cremated.)

As anybody knows, the whole thing begins with an assault on the body, usually when someone slaps us on the arse to get the breath going. The first one being an inhalation, and the last one being an elusive exhalation with corpse-to-be vainly trying to recapture it and funnel it back to the lungs.

The mother born Angela Sheehan on January 1, 1908, took her first breath in Limerick, Ireland, and from her descriptions of her life, all her breaths from then on were uneasy. She smoked cigarettes from the age of thirteen. She gave birth to seven children, three of whom died in childhood from various respiratory failures, perhaps because of the constant presence of cigarette smoke in their short lives. She panted, she wheezed, and she coughed for many years because she had severe and chronic bronchitis and, finally, emphysema. Angela was a walking advertisement for the stop-smoking brigade.

The day arrived when she could walk no more and had to have oxygen administered all the days of her life and, indeed, all the hours too.

Then it was off to Lenox Hill Hospital in New York City, where she was hooked up to various life-sustaining devices. One of the questions asked her was, "What did your husband do?" She could not think of the phrase *jack-of-all-trades,* so she said he was an "all-round man." "All-round what?" they asked. She said, "All round the bars." Her reputation as a wit was established in the hospital, and thus she got very good treatment.

As death approached, her moods changed and depression set in. A psychiatrist was dispatched to her bedside, and after a few perfunctory questions he informed her that, in his opinion, she was depressed. She told him that that was a coincidence, as she was of the same opinion, but wouldn't he be depressed if he were on the verge of death, and were sick, so miserable they wouldn't let him die? They allow abortions, but insist on keeping people alive who don't want to live. She told the psychiatrist to go and help someone who needed to live. A Catholic priest arrived, and she waved him off, as the church had not been of much help when she was trying to raise four children alone in Catholic Ireland.

I was having a fiftieth birthday party and, against all medical advice, she heaved herself out of the bed into a wheelchair and got herself to the party venue and distinguished herself by being the only dying person present. One of our friends at the party, Bernard Carabello, said to her, "I hope you don't die during the party." "Why?" said she. "Because I couldn't stand the excitement," Bernard replied. She reassured him that she had to get back to the hospital and did not want to disappoint the nursing staff by dying off premises. She returned to the hospital and resumed her intake of pills, medication, and, most importantly, oxygen.

As the days passed, her medical condition worsened, and she kept wondering why they would not allow her to die. They shushed her and told her not to talk like that. The situation was not helped by her bingo friends, who kept telling her that she would be out and about for Christmas and back to bingo. They all knew she was dying, but people play games when death is looming.

I requested a meeting with the main physician to discuss how we could let her go. He hemmed and hawed about getting her to a nursing home, how it was against the ethics of medicine and against the law to assist in a person's dying. I don't know why I said it or what it means, but out of my mouth it came. "Don't worry, Doctor. You see, we come from a long line of dead people."

The doctor looked like a man who has just been cornered by a pack of rabid dogs. He gasped something about Code Red or Code Blue or some emergency, and he fled down the hall, away from this non sequitur–spouting lunatic. Later on that day, the nursing staff did remove the intravenous needles, leaving only the oxygen to facilitate comfortable breathing.

The family gathered about to make the final farewells, and so began the deathwatch as she sank into what is commonly called a coma. At about two in the morning, I was seated in the chair at the foot of her bed, listening to her labored breathing. At one point, she opened one eye and observed me. "What are you doing here?" said she.

"I thought you might die this night!" said I.

"I might and I might not," said she, "but that is my business, so why don't you go home to your bed?"

Which is what I did, and at about 5 AM the telephone rang, and the voice at the other end informed me that the mother had just died. She had an innate courtesy, which would not allow her to die while someone was visiting her, and that's why she waited till I was gone.

Brothers Frank, Alphie, and Mike and myself met with a funeral undertaker who was festooned with things gold: gold watch, gold spectacles, gold tie clip, gold rings, gold tie pin, gold teeth, and highly polished fingernails. His golden tanned face was set in practiced commercial condolence. He sat behind a desk, elbows propped, fingertips together cathedral-style, saying things like, "You will want the redwood casket with the blue satin lining and the brass handles." Our reply was, "No, we will not want that one, as we are cremating her, and could we possibly have a body bag for the purpose? And while we are at it, is it possible to have her collected by the sanitation department?"

The gold-bedecked undertaker did not appreciate the levity and left the room to recover from the inappropriate witticisms of a bunch of Irish sons who had no respect for undertakers or for death itself. My brother Alphie, usually the quiet one—thus dubbed *chatterbox* by the ironic mother—remarked,

"There goes a man well experienced in extreme unctuousness," a pun that sent us into the heights of hilarity, the state that happens only at times of sorrow.

Angela was cremated without ceremony and her ashes returned to us in what appeared to be the kind of can that is used to contain peas. Whilst bringing her ashes to Ireland, the aeroplane sprung a leak in one of the doors. The high-pitched piercing whistle from that leak was deafening, and to calm the frightened passengers I asked if anyone would like to meet my mother. Some said yes and I produced the can, holding up her ashes and announcing, "Here she is!" For some reason, people on planes that have to return to aeroports because of trouble do not want to meet dead people in flight, so introducing them to my mother was a social failure.

We did eventually get to Ireland and put Angela's ashes in her old family graveyard. We had to sneak them in, due to the graveyard being part of a tenth-century abbey, which is now a preserved national monument; no more burials are allowed. As we stood there, this family of McCourts, we did laugh a lot, and we did sing first of all the songs that Angela disliked, as we felt she might pull a phoenix act and arise from the ashes and tell us to shut up, and then we sang the songs she liked, including "Will Ye Go, Lassie, Go," and she went.

And that was end of Angela McCourt on this planet.

In the middle of spring, in what should have been the middle of his life, my husband died, leaving me and three young sons, as well as a teen daughter from a previous marriage. Nothing about this was good.

Although all the morphine that hospice could give finally was unable to quell the pain so that Dan could sleep or even talk with his siblings or the children, he did not long for "peace." The end was preferable only in that there is no fighting colon cancer once it digs in its talons. We lived then in Madison, Wisconsin, and at his memorial, when people told six-year-old Danny that his father was in "a better place," Danny explained that Dan really preferred Dane County to heaven.

As memorial services go, it was a good one. Although his sister was enraged that we didn't opt for a Catholic mass (for Dan hated standard-issue Catholicism with all the passion of a former altar boy), one of the privileges of widowhood (along with no longer having to send Christmas cards) is not giving a big damn what other people think. All Dan's friends came, and all his enemies came, too. As a crusading political reporter, Dan took the journalistic adjuration about afflicting

the comfortable utterly seriously; but even the immensely pop-
ular Republican governor paid a visit, later telling me that he
and Dan had their differences but that Dan always fought fair,
and cherishing family was something on which they agreed.
The big Frank Lloyd Wright meetinghouse was filled with
the music Dan had loved—and music was his passion—from
"God Only Knows" to "Ashokan Farewell."

And then, because Dan never did anything according to
standard procedure, after the funeral, his best friends—among
them Michael and Mad Dog (I didn't know Mad Dog's real
name until twenty years later)—hosted his wake. There were
fireworks. There were lots of fireworks, and staid neighbors
who might have been apt to complain came instead to join
the fun. I had my first two or six shots of whiskey (and I was
nearly forty years old!) and promptly got outrageously sick.
I can remember my brother telling me that if anyone could
see me, they would be appalled by my throwing up like a dog
eating grass. However, not then or now have I had a stomach
for liquor. I went home early with my brother, my father, and
the boys, who were only four, six, and ten, to put off for one
more day facing the Big Question: how I was going to support
the kids. All the life insurance Dan had amounted to a 1993
year's salary for a small-town newspaper editor.

So I wasn't there for the gigantic thunderstorm that rolled
in late. I didn't hear the story of what happened to four of
Dan's closest friends until much later. When I heard, I could
not stop laughing—and again, I didn't care who knew it. At
first, I felt pretty invulnerable, as fools will.

The earliest five or six months for a widow (not a widower) are pretty great. Families offer to make room at picnics and fishing excursions for your kids. And then, although men raising kids as an only parent continue to receive the sweetest strokes and comeliest casseroles, an odd-woman-out becomes something of a burden and even something of a threat. Friends drifted away, some with no explanation, some just confessing that they didn't know what to do for me.

One Friday night, when I called my friend Laurie to ask if she and her three kids could get together with us, she gave me what obviously had been the piece of her mind she'd been holding back. "We have husbands and families, Jackie," she said. "We can't drop everything and do something with you anymore." I was heartbroken, and my relationship with Laurie never was the same, but I got it. The circus of Dan's early, fast, and horrific death had moved on. My friendships now would be fewer, much fewer, because not only the couple friends but the single friends would fade away, one sort of afraid of the contagion, one a little miffed that my posse had to go wherever I went.

But this recognition was far in the future, and I still believed that people loved me not only for myself but for my sufferings.

After Dan's wake, the house party was rained indoors, but three of Dan's closest friends from town, along with another from out of town, decided to go up to the roof of the Mendota Mental Health Institute—the place in the State of Wisconsin where the severely mentally ill live, sometimes all their lives. Ed Gein, whose affection for his mother inspired

Robert Bloch's novel *Psycho*, had died not long before at Mendota. Ed's favorite part of his week were the Thursday night mixers, because Ed, murderer of at least two women besides his mother, did like the ladies. Dan's good friend, Ken, was a psychiatrist and the administrator of Mendota.

There was a covered area on the roof, and Ken led three other friends up there to watch the lightning over one of Madison's three city lakes. They talked about old times and how much Dan would have loved the thunderstorm. As news channels screamed for families to take cover in tornadoes, he was always outside with his old camera, hoping to capture a real twister on film. That night, the storm was more sound than real fury, and after an hour or so, the friends made their way down. Dan's best friend, Rob, had to go back to New York the following morning, and the others had pressing business as well.

When they strolled up to the gate, flanked by ten-foot fences with electrified razor wire on top, the night watchman asked pleasantly, "And where are you gentlemen headed?"

Later, Ken would wonder if the storm had interrupted the electrical current, but the man's manner was polite and calm. Similarly politely and calmly, Ken reached into his jeans pocket for his ID. But he'd left it in the car. Reasonably, Ken explained that he'd just been to a great friend's funeral and now he needed to go home. He added that he was the medical director of Mendota. Why the man on duty at midnight should have believed this was anyone's guess, but Ken was still surprised when the gatekeeper said, "You are, huh?"

"He is!" spoke up Dan's closest friend from work. "And I'm the editor of the newspaper!"

Rick added, "I'm the Dane County executive!"

And not to be outdone, Rob said, "I'm a columnist for the *New York Times!*"

"You are, huh?" repeated the watchman, who had by then summoned several others.

No one could stop laughing—they realized how absurd they sounded—until the guard offered to escort them back inside, nice and friendly-like. Ken protested, spluttering. But spluttering is what a delusional person does best, and it was a good two hours before Ken could give his keys to someone who fetched his wallet with its ID, and until all the others' IDs were verified, and double-verified, with calls to the police, the executive editor of the local paper, and the *New York Times,* where the guy on the desk at first had no idea who Rob was.

When they finally left, in the wee hours of a cold spring morning, Rob, the most fanciful and sentimental of the group said, "Dan gave us all a lot of laughs. That was his last laugh on us."

They all agreed. It was just the kind of story Dan would have loved to hear.

They hoped he had.

UP HERE

— Amy Ferris —

She must have a window seat. This, she promises, is her last phone call for the night, reminding me one more time, *"It must be a window seat."* I tell her, "I will do my best. The plane seems awfully full, and since it's a last-minute booking, it might be hard."

"If I tell you I want a window seat, get me a window seat." Click.

This phone exchange was not long after she had been diagnosed with moderate-stage dementia. She had some scary moments—unsettling, jarring, completely-out-of-left-field confusing moments. While visiting for a long weekend, my husband, Ken, and I found her curled up in a ball, naked on the floor in her bedroom in Florida. She had absolutely no recollection of how she landed there. When I shook her from her sound sleep, she smiled and told me I looked a lot taller than she remembered. "Ma, you're on the floor."

"Oh. It feels comfy though; you sure it's the floor?"

There were the middle-of-the-night phone calls when she thought it was the middle of the day; there were the panicked phone calls about her bank account. She had stopped balancing her checkbook, and believed she was being "robbed." And then there were the phone calls wondering why my dad hadn't returned from the bagel place when, in fact, my father had died a few years earlier.

She was becoming much more agitated, much more impatient, and much less vain. Bathing became a chore for her. Losing her keys became second nature. Burning toast was a daily routine.

A bat mitzvah in Scarsdale, New York, galvanized her into major travel frenzy. She wanted desperately to go. A spur-of-the-minute decision, literally.

"I have to go. I have to see Gertie. I have to go."

Gertie was her older sister. Theirs was a relationship not dissimilar to Palestine and Israel.

"I have to go. Don't tell me I'm not going." The thing about my mom was she was as stubborn as the day was long. God's honest truth, sometimes it was really hard to tell if it was the dementia or my mother just being herself.

"Ma, I don't think it's a good idea, you traveling by yourself."

"Oh, really? Fine. I'll drive to Gert's," she proposed after she had rammed her car into a fire hydrant—a glaring sign that she should never be behind the wheel, ever again—a few weeks earlier. "It came out of nowhere," she said. "One minute I was sitting there, minding my own business, and the next minute, there it was, crossing the street."

What do you say? *Really?* "Ma, it can't walk. A fire hydrant doesn't walk."

Unfortunately, having her car keys taken away from her required more than just a sit-down—removing them from her grip required the jaws-of-life. It is, I learned, the last bit of true freedom and independence, and it is never given up without a fight.

I worked it out so a car service (a very kind man who lived a few doors down from her) would come and pick her up, drop her off at the JetBlue terminal, and make sure there were no seen *or unforeseen* problems. I paid the guy to wait an extra half hour. I called the airline and spoke with a reservation agent, who had just the right combination of humor and sympathy and could not have been any more cordial or kind. She promised that they would do whatever they could to accommodate my mom, but she needed to remind me that the plane was, in fact, full, and hopefully someone would be able to move, since there was not a window seat available. I asked her if there was a "companion" person—a representative—who could help my mom get settled, help her with her boarding pass, and handle the other unexpected frustrations that might arise.

"Yes," she said, "someone will help your mom." I hoped and prayed for my mother to come face-to-face with kindness. I thought of all the times I gave up a window seat for an elderly person, or a pregnant woman, or a wife who wanted to sit next to her husband. I was hopeful.

Standing outside her condo with a massive suitcase and an overnight bag, having packed enough clothing for an entire month or lifetime, whichever came first, she was picked up at the designated time. "Maybe I'll stay for a few extra weeks," she had told me the night before, when she listed all the clothing she was bringing. I heard in her voice something I had never heard before: loneliness.

She got to the JetBlue terminal and checked her suitcase

outside with baggage claim, and (the neighbor/car service driver told me) handed a crisp ten-dollar bill to the bag handler, telling him he was a lovely, lovely kind man. He deeply appreciated her gesture. Little did he know that the remaining ten or so crisp ten- and twenty-dollar bills that she had tucked ever so neatly into her wallet would make their way to others who smiled, offered a hand, let her get ahead in line, and helped her with her carry-on.

She made her way up to the counter, where a ticket should be waiting for her. Yes, the agent told her, there was a ticket, but she must go to the gate in order to get a window seat.

She went through the whole security scene, and I am told by the neighbor/car service guy about the taking off of her shoes, the removing of her belt, the telling of a joke or two about her hip replacement *after she in fact set off the security alarm* and how the sound once reminded her of the old days in Las Vegas when someone won at the slots, and it was a sound filled with "good wishes."

"No more," she said loudly, as if telling it to every single person on the security line. "It's a phony sound. It has no heart. Gimme back my shoes."

The neighbor/car service guy could not go any farther with my mom. The rules. The companion person from JetBlue now met her, thankfully.

There was no window seat available. She had an aisle seat. No one wanted to give up a seat.

This is where I get to relive the whole crazy scenario as it was repeated to me, beat by beat, blow by excruciating blow. My mother threw a shit storm of a nut-dance, flung a racial slur at the African American flight attendant, and then, if that weren't enough, caused another passenger who was somewhat overweight to break down and cry. "You know how fat you are? You have your own zip code."

She was escorted off the plane, and somehow managed to get back to her condo by renting a car, even though she had an expired license. I would just love to meet the Avis rental person who gave my mom a red Mustang to tool around in.

She called me in absolute hyper-hysterics. She wanted me to fire every single one of those nasty, bitchy flight attendants, and pilots, and the copilot—he was as much to blame. And where was her luggage, her *fucking* luggage? "I bet they stole it. They stole it and you should fire them, the whole lot of them. Now. I want you to fire them now."

"Okay, Ma. I'm gonna fire them now."

I found out from another very cordial and patient JetBlue rep that her luggage was on its way to New York. I was in Los Angeles on business; my brother was at a birthday celebration on Long Island. Neither one of us had expected this hailstorm. I tried to deal with the airport bureaucracy and arranged for my mom's luggage to make its way to Fort Lauderdale within forty-eight hours, barring no glitches.

The administrator on the phone told me it was like an unstoppable chaotic ruckus, a tornado, a whirlwind. "Your mother is old and frail and disruptive."

Holy shit.

I felt sad. I felt horribly sad and, dare I say, embarrassed, wholly, deeply, immensely embarrassed, because this old frail woman is, in fact, *my mom.*

"While we really appreciate your business, we must inform you that your mother, Beatrice, will no longer be able to fly with us."

This did not surprise me. I told the JetBlue representative that my mom has the beginning stages of dementia. It comes and goes, but mostly it's coming these days. I gave her all the broad strokes—my dad died, she's living alone, we know, we know, it's time to get her settled, she's stubborn, she's independent, and there's the whole question of what to do now. Move her, or does she stay? And she's always been much more strident and righteous and defiant. Not going gently into the good night.

For the record, every single JetBlue employee I spoke to knew exactly what happened on that plane. They not only knew all about my mother's tantrum but, just like the game telephone, each and every time I spoke with someone new there seemed to be an added bit of shocking information. I was waiting for someone to tell me she stormed the cockpit, demanding to fly the plane to New York. I can only imagine the watercooler conversation about the crazy woman and the window seat.

My mother refused to speak to anyone. She felt duped and lied to and thought that the fat girl should have gotten up. "My God, she took up two goddamn seats." And then she said, "I always, always have to sit at the window." *"Why,"* I asked her, *"why?"*

"Fuck you," she hung up on me.

Trying to calm my mother down was near impossible. And just like the JetBlue employees, my mother's version of the story became more and more exaggerated and embellished each and every time she told it—repeated it, shared it. By the time I spoke with my cousin Carol, my mother was claiming she was strip-searched and held prisoner in a room, naked ... *without a television.*

"Without a television?" my cousin asked her, feigning shock and awe.

"Yes, that's correct, I couldn't watch my shows."

"I'm so sorry, Aunt Bea. That must've been so hard and difficult."

"Yes, it was. But they gave me a private airplane and ten million dollars."

Dementia is filled with surprises. Unfiltered surprises. It is an unwanted visitor with a selective memory.

Shortly thereafter, I moved my mom to New Mexico, not far from my brother, where she was about to start living in an assisted-living facility.

When we arrived at the Fort Lauderdale airport, I witnessed her interaction with the bag handler at baggage claim. After he took her luggage and placed it on the conveyor belt, she handed him a crisp ten-dollar bill, telling him, "You're a lovely, lovely man." He was mighty appreciative of her generosity. I witnessed her stepping through security with the alarm going off, because of her hip replacement, and her retelling the same joke about the Vegas slot machines to all and anyone who would listen and laugh. It made her feel important, valued. It added a little bounce to her walk. And as we walked to the gate, I sensed the first stages of panic; it was there, in her eyes. Right there in her eyes, a bit of worry and fear.

She stopped and looked at me. "Did you get me a window seat?"

"Yeah, Ma, I got you a window seat."

"Really? You did?"

"Yeah."

"Good," she said. "Good."

As the plane revved up its engines and was about to take off, my mom took my hand and squeezed it. Staring out the window, watching the plane disappear into the gorgeous white clouds, she turned to me after a few long moments and said, "Up here in the clouds, I can dream all I want." Then she pointed to two clouds, almost intertwined, and she said with such joy, "See that. See that. They're dancing together. Just like Daddy and me. You can only see this kind of magic from a window seat."

In that moment, on that plane, the lines on her face smoothed out, and her eyes filled with remembrance, as if every memory were intact. A twinkle. She started to giggle. She was so very happy, content—an awakening of sorts.

"Thank you so much," she said. "You don't know how much this means to me."

It was here that my mother had always been able to see and feel and imagine clouds dancing, forms taking shape, lovers kissing, the intertwining of souls, and as her hand pressed up against the window, she could feel the kindness of heaven.

Not long after, she died.

KITTY... MIMI

— Karen Quinn —

The days following September 11, 2001, were painful for my children, made even more so by the fact that a beloved family member died just a week later at their mother's hand. Schuyler was ten and Sam was nine on that clear, crisp morning when jets flew into the World Trade Center. We lived in a twenty-first-floor apartment on Union Square that had postcard views of the Twin Towers from our bedroom and office. It was one of the features that had attracted us to the place.

I strolled toward home after dropping the kids at school, unaware that anything was amiss. Had I looked up I would have seen it, but I didn't. As I neared home, I ran into Susan, a parent at the school who would soon get breast cancer, although we did not know it then. Susan told me about her daughter's new hypoallergenic poodle, a concept I had never heard of. Little did we know as we talked that Susan would never make it home that day because she lived across from the World Trade Center, and that her poodle would have to be rescued by the building's superintendent and held until Susan and her family could get back into their apartment to retrieve him.

This is what I do after a tragedy: I think about the moments before it happened and envy my innocent self, the one that didn't know that her life was about to suffer irreparably and could never be put back to the way it was before.

Once home, I entered my bedroom, glanced at the TV that was on, and caught images of the World Trade Center, both towers fully engulfed in flames. In a surreal moment, I looked out the window and saw the same scene taking place just blocks away. I screamed for my husband, who was in the shower, as oblivious to the disaster as I had been on my walk home. "Mark, turn off the water! The World Trade Center's on fire!" It didn't occur to me that the buildings were so far apart that a fire in one would not engulf the other. My mind registered *one fire* and *one World Trade Center*, and I couldn't begin to fathom the reality of how two separate attacks had taken place during the time it took me to walk my children to school, talk to a few parents, and return home. I crumpled to the floor and watched the TV instead of looking out the window, focused on Katie Couric explaining what had happened—something about plane crashes and a possible attack.

Before Mark emerged from the bathroom, I was up and out the door again, off to retrieve the children at school. It seemed like the right thing to do. This time I ran, arriving at the front door of Friends Seminary just as they were locking everyone in. "Wait, I want my kids!" I cried to the woman who normally worked in the lower school office.

"We're not letting anyone leave," she explained. "We think the kids are safer at school."

I didn't argue. Nothing like this had ever happened, and if the school wanted to lock my children in during a national emergency instead of give them back to me, I didn't think to disagree with them. What to do? I wondered.

Then I remembered that we had no food in the house. One of my dearest friends had gotten married the weekend before in Southampton, and the whole family had been there. In fact, I'd shared Sunday brunch with a friend of the bride who at that very moment was trapped inside the Windows of the World restaurant on the 103rd floor of the north tower and would soon die, if he hadn't already. I didn't know that yet. All I knew was that we were out of milk, and I should go shopping before everyone else got the same idea.

In the days that followed, my children did not cry, nor did they want to talk about what happened. We kept the TV off to spare them the horrific images, but they could not ignore what had taken place. Every night there were candlelight vigils across the street in Union Square for the lost or dead. Wherever you ventured, flyers containing photos of loved ones who had left for work that day and never returned home were posted with "MISSING" written beneath them. The children understood that something was very wrong in the world. "Why is everyone being so nice to each other?" Sam asked, unused to a kinder, gentler, wounded New York City.

Though they did not express their feelings, I recognized my children's pain. Sam would tote his pillow and blanket into my room in the middle of the night and sleep on the floor; Schuyler would bring our cat, Kitty, into her bed for comfort.

Kitty was a Maine coon that our doorman, Richard, had

rescued a year earlier. He and the concierge had put her in a box from the A&P and shown her to each resident who walked by, hoping someone would take her in. The kids met her before I did, and it was desperation for a pet at first sight. "Please, Mom," they begged. "We'll take care of her. We love her *so* much." I had my doubts. Cats had never appealed to me. Mark, who wanted no part of a dog, was willing to give her a try. "Cats are easier than dogs," he reasoned. "No walking. No barking. Why not?"

Why not, indeed? She was such a beautiful cat that we were sure she must have escaped from another family that loved her. Though we put up signs all over the neighborhood reading "FOUND–CAT" with her picture, no one ever claimed her. It didn't take long before she wiggled her way into our hearts.

We discovered that if you held catnip slightly behind her head, she would do as many as eight backward flips in a row until she "caught" it. Our humidifier became her nemesis. She would stalk it for hours, pouncing each time a bubble gurgled up through the water bottle. In the days following 9/11, Kitty was a source of comfort to the children. She would crawl into their laps and curl into a warm, purring ball they could hold and love and that reassured each of them in their own innocent way that everything would be okay again.

About a week after the disaster, Mark went on a business trip. I don't remember where. He flew out on one of the first days the airports were open and told me he practically had the plane to himself. I didn't want him to leave us, but life had begun to move on. School was open again. I went back to work. Mark had meetings to attend.

The night he left town, the children and I were watching TV in the living room. The telephone rang. It was Richard, the doorman. "Karen, do you know where your cat is?" he said.

"Of course, I do," I said, my stomach flipping the way stomachs do when you fear something terrible has happened. Did I really know where she was? Was she where she was supposed to be? "Why do you ask?"

"Well, we found a cat's body down here and it might be Kitty . . ."

I dropped the phone and rushed to my office where I caught sight of the window, which was directly above my desk. Though I remembered leaving it open a few inches, it was now fully ajar. I knew instantly that Kitty had jumped onto my desk and nudged it open to go outside. She was always trying to escape. I could only guess that she had ventured out to the slim ledge and fallen to her death when she turned to come back inside.

As I ran through the living room to the front door, my kids looked up. "What's going on?" they asked. "Nothing," I said. "I have to go check on something."

I felt nauseous riding the elevator down. How could we lose Kitty? Not when the kids needed her so. A thick lump formed in my throat as I held back tears. I loved Kitty as much as the children did. How could I have been so careless? It was unforgivable.

By the time I reached the front desk, Richard had gone on his dinner break. No one could find anyone who knew anything about finding a cat's body. Finally, someone paged the custodian. "Oh, yes," he confirmed. "We found a dead cat. I wrapped it in a Hefty bag and threw it away."

"You threw it away?" I cried. "You couldn't wait to find her family? Where is she?"

The custodian walked me outside and pointed to a mountain of stuffed black Hefty bags on the corner, waiting to be picked up the next day. "It's in there," he said. "You can look for it if you want, but I'm not digging through that."

Somewhere in that mound of trash was Kitty. Did I want to break open each bag searching for her corpse? No. But would I do it for my children who were about to be crushed with this terrible news, my children who needed some closure? Would I dig through mounds of waste until I found our cat's remains, the way firefighters at Ground Zero were still searching for the fallen? No, I decided. I could not bear to do that.

Defeated, I retreated upstairs to tell my children the news.

"Where is her body?" Schuyler asked. "We have to have a funeral."

"That's the good news," I lied. "They took her upstate for burial in a wonderful cat cemetery."

My kids actually believed I had made funeral arrangements that quickly, but that didn't satisfy them. "Cat murderer!" Schuyler accused, when I admitted that it had been my office window from which she had leapt. "You have Kitty's blood on your hands."

"I hate you!" my son cried.

Both children wept and let their emotions loose in a way that had eluded them in the days after 9/11. "Our cat is gone!"

Schuyler cried, tears streaming down her cheeks. "What are we going to do? How are we going to live? How could you let her die? You're the grown-up. You're supposed to know better." Schuyler sobbed in tremendous heaves until she threw up.

"We will never forgive you," Sam said, shaking his head sadly. That night, he whimpered like a kitten in his sleep as he crashed at the foot of my bed.

I tried to call Mark's hotel, to let him know what had happened. It had been an accident. I wanted him to hear about it from me and not from Richard when he returned home. Each time I called, however, I missed him. Neither of us had a cell phone back then. He'd return the call, and I wouldn't be home. I'd call the hotel, and he would be out. For three days this went on. I was living with my children's grief and their anger at me, trying to get through to my husband, but not connecting with the one person who would offer me comfort and forgiveness. First the World Trade Center, then Kitty. It had been a devastating two weeks.

On Friday night, the phone rang. It was Mark calling from the airport. He had just arrived and was waiting for his luggage.

"Oh, thank God," I said at the sound of his voice. "I've been trying to reach you for days. Something terrible has happened."

I could feel Mark tense through the phone. "What happened?" he said. "Who died?"

"Kitty," I said, bursting with the news. *"Kitty died."*

Mark was surprisingly calm. "Well, that's expected," he said. "At least she lived a good life."

Although I did not know it then, when I told Mark that

Kitty died, what he heard was, "Mimi died." Mimi was my ninety-nine-year-old grandmother. She was living on the ground floor of an old folks' home in San Antonio, Texas. For the past two years, she had suffered from dementia. To Mark, her death was a blessing.

"How can you say her death is expected?" I cried. "It's a shock."

"Not really. What happened?" Mark asked.

"She jumped out the window and died!" I explained.

As I spoke these words, Mark imagined Mimi jumping out the first floor window of her retirement home and dying. "So it was suicide," he said. "She must have been awfully fragile to die from a fall like that."

"Suicide?" I said. "No, it was an accident. And of course, she died. Who wouldn't die from a fall like that?"

From the first floor? he was thinking. "When is the funeral?" he asked.

I erupted into tears. "That's the terrible part," I wailed. "The maintenance man wrapped her body in a Hefty bag and threw it in the trash for the trashmen to pick up."

"What?" Mark cried. "Is that how they do things in Texas?"

"Texas?" I said. "What are you talking about? This happened in Manhattan."

"Mimi came to Manhattan?" Mark asked. "I thought she couldn't travel. And then she fell from a window?"

"No, not Mimi," I said, "KITTY. Kitty fell from the window. She's dead. They threw her away."

"Kitty? Not Mimi? Oh, dear God, *no*," he said, his voice thick with shock. "I can't believe it."

At that moment, I realized what Mark had been thinking all along, and I started to laugh. "Oh, my God! Oh, my God! You thought . . . you actually thought . . ." The laughter was such a relief after so many days of mourning and sadness. The image of ninety-nine-year-old Mimi jumping out the first-floor window of her retirement home and the maintenance man wrapping her little body in a Hefty bag and tossing it in the trash was all it took to put me over the edge.

For a moment, I forgot about Kitty. I forgot about the World Trade Center. I laughed and laughed—big, deep belly laughs that made all the pain disappear, at least for a short time.

Even Mark, who was devastated by Kitty's death, couldn't help but laugh about our "Who's on First" conversation. For a few minutes, we both escaped the pain and grief of two heartbreaking events—one in the life of the world, the other in the life of our family. I knew then that everything would be okay again. Different, but okay.

A few years later, Mimi passed in her sleep. When I heard my aunt on the other end of the phone say "Mimi died," I smiled, remembering a moment that had illuminated the darkest and most difficult of days.

A COLD AWAKENING

— *Dianne Rinehart* —

I'm looking down on him now. His face has just a trace of a smile, somehow. How do they do that? I wonder.

Now I'm looking at his jacket collar. It bears the Royal Canadian Air Force pin he's always been so proud to wear.

He is a man of modest means, so the suit reflects a man dressed up, but not one who is wealthy.

At this first sighting of my father in his coffin, I'm filled with grief, not judgment. That will come later, in arguments with my siblings about *who* was to blame for what we endured.

But for now, my heart is breaking, and the tears are flowing. Why?

How could he have been out dancing Saturday night with his girlfriend—the love of his life, he has told me—and then gone home to prepare a birthday party for my mother the next day and, instead, be found dead in his bed that morning by my very frightened younger brother, Mikey?

When my father doesn't answer the buzzer at his condo, Michael, his wife, and young children, who've arrived first for my mother's party, go up to his apartment. No answer at their knock. Worried my father has taken ill, Michael tries his key, but for the first time ever, it won't let him in. They finally give up and leave, but on the way home, his wife Kim says she thinks something is wrong. They turn back. This time the kids stay in the car with her, and he heads up alone.

The key turns magically and effortlessly in the lock—in the immediate aftermath, we ask ourselves if it's possible that Dad's spirit stopped the key from turning when Michael's kids were at the door—and Michael heads toward our dad's bedroom. He knows that he's not going to like what he sees. One glance and he explodes out of the building to get his wife. She goes up with him, warning their frightened children to stay in the car, doors locked.

"That's dead, that's dead, isn't it!?" Michael asks, hysterically running from one side of the bed to the other. Our father has died in his sleep, his hands folded prayerlike, with his face resting on them, as if they are his pillow, as he always did when he was snoozing. (This image of my sweet younger brother leaping around the room saying "That's dead, that's dead, isn't it!?" will become part of the black humor my older brother and I engage throughout the long goodbye services to break our heartache.)

But for now I'm not laughing.

"How could you leave without saying goodbye?" I choke out to him in the funeral parlor, where my siblings have left me for a private moment with him, minutes after I've arrived from Ottawa, driving for hours through a relentless, pouring rain.

He was so vibrant, so engaged by life, books, people, humor.

He was so alive—so much more so than my mother, who has been dying from a million paper cuts her entire life and now resides in a nursing home—that when my brother-in-law calls me the day before to tell me my father is dead, I respond, "You mean my mother."

"No, your father."

"No, you mean my mother."

He repeats the news again, insistently.

It's unbelievable.

We always thought she of frail health, she of bitterness instead of joy—a woman you could find in her nightclothes any time of day, she'd so given up on living, never mind going out—would die first.

It was our belief that when she died, my father could truly come alive, live without her hitting him over the head with guilt because she, a war bride, was only in Canada to please *him*, as if he'd kidnapped her, rather than married her.

And now, he's not going to get the chance to experience that freedom from a lifetime of bitterness and guilt. And I will never get the answer from him that I've been quietly asking for the past few years, since our family had that single session with a family psychiatrist: *why?*

I'm thirteen, boyish, and small for my age, and somehow—though I do hours of chores each week, complete my homework without being asked, and am irrepressibly cheery—I've done something to upset my mother... again. The constant hammering of her outbursts that morning make me react as I've never done before. I don't think, I act: I am about to fight back. "You're a witch!" I protest childishly, not in defiance, but frustration. And then I'm shocked at the effect of these defiant words, when shame and supplication is what she is used to. "Get her, Norm!" she commands.

Over the decades, those words will stick. It's like my dad is an attack dog, and she is siccing him on me, as she will many times throughout my teenage years.

And he leaps to her command. His face erupts in fury. (I will later realize that this is from his own impotence in life, not anything I've done.) He chases me down the hall to my bedroom, where I try to shut him out—then run to . . . where? The bed. There's nowhere else to go.

His fists pummel me until he's sated. Punched senseless. I stagger to school, reeling not from the wounds that will be repeated time and again—the ones that will turn into visible bruises so often that my guidance counselor offers to have me taken from my home and placed in a shelter for young girls—but from those no one will see.

This first beating is different. This isn't the spanking we all got as kids, whacks delivered by him with brushes and belts almost always at her command, or her own beatings, when we were very small, when she'd snatch us by our hair, force us to the ground, then kick us in the stomach. I didn't need combat training to learn the importance of the fetal position. Or him forcing us awake on a Saturday to do hours of chores, driving us from the warmth of our beds by soaking a washcloth under freezing water, then pulling down our covers and sloshing it over us. This is him *losing* it and punching out all his frustrations in life on all ninety pounds of me.

But I'm too young to understand; I think it's me, as I always do when she lashes out.

Once, when she comes home from a dance with my father, she takes off her stilettos at the doorway and belts one, totally without warning, clear across the room at me. I go from standing up from the sofa in a slumber to survival mode, ducking just in time to see the shoe embed itself for an endless second in the plaster wall behind me, rather than my eye socket. In a movie, I'd have a quick comeback, delivered deadpan: "You could poke someone's eye out with that, you know."

Another time, I'm watching TV in the same room with her, and like a stealth bomber she attacks from nowhere. One minute she's lying on the sofa, the next she's throwing a heavy glass ashtray at me. It sails a good fifteen feet and connects cleanly with the glass of Coke I'm raising to my lips at that moment. Focused on some ridiculous comedy show (I'm not making this up), I didn't see this one coming. I only hear the glass shattering and feel the pieces flying into my face, a thousand tiny pieces cutting into my skin. Thankfully, again, not my eyes.

The U.S. military could have used her when they developed the guidance system for their so-called smart bombs, the ones that, unlike my mother, so often miss their targets.

Decades later, I don't know whether to thank the gods for her innate athleticism or curse them. Who else could throw an ashtray or stiletto across the room with such precision? But if her aim was off, would the damage to my body, as opposed to my heart, have been worse? I will also begin to see it through a more informed view hammered out from the healing of time and the understandings that come with age and experience: I am haunted not so much anymore by my own pain but hers.

What frustration, heartbreak, and fears could have caused her to lash out like that?

But right then, right there, I think only, as all beaten children do: it's me. It must be something that I'm doing.

So I keep trying.

One year I rent a cottage with my then-husband on a gorgeous lake, and I want my parents to experience the beauty of it. They never get out, never mind vacation. I'm determined that if I can just give them this, *everything* will change.

I've also bought, though I have little money, tickets to the local town play, but something I say on the way to the theater makes my mother angry. She goes silent, and her face forms that familiar terrorizing mask that warns of *so* much more to come, and fills us with dread. But I'm not about to give up. I was so excited to be showing them this play, buying them a drink like other families that, unlike us, go to events, drive through a picturesque town alongside a sparkling lake, and share a cottage. I simply want them to enjoy it. I want her to be happy.

I keep trying.

But now she is punishing me for whatever I've said that offended her, by not speaking throughout the entire evening.

After the play, we drive home in silence, and she storms wordlessly into the bedroom I've given them—the one with the comfortable bed—and I can't bear it anymore. I've tried so hard. I leave the cottage sobbing so hard I'm choking. My husband, helplessly (who can blame him, since I've barely hinted at my family secrets?) retires, but my father, surprisingly, comes out.

"It's not her fault, it's mine," he says, as I stand . . . absolutely stunned.

It's the first time he's even hinted, never mind acknowledged, that something isn't right in her responses.

And then he begins, unbelievably, to tell me the ways he has disappointed *her* over the years. It will be many years before I begin to see her behavior in the light of this: a woman who felt she had no control, a woman who lashed out because of fear, not necessarily anger.

On this night of pain, juxtaposed against this pristine lakeside setting with crickets singing, my father is giving me the first tools I need to heal. Later, I'll recognize this as his biggest gift: the whisper of a beginning to understand that it wasn't me, it was her. And the things about her were not my fault; I could not have prevented them.

The words spill out of him that night, and only that night, and only with me. My other siblings hear none of this. He's had affairs. Not one. Many. And he begins to tell me about some of the women. At that moment, I want to hold my hands over my ears. I don't want to hear this about my dad. He's always been blameless in our eyes: not hitting us because he wanted to, but because she *made* him.

Now he's telling me about the woman who was so petite. He sounds happy reminiscing about her. She wanted to hold his hand all the time.

Later, as an adult who's experienced her own heartache, I will think about his lover and how she might have thought he'd leave his wife for her, and whether she blamed herself or him when it ended, because he literally went home one night to my mother with lipstick on his collar. That put a stop to the affair, he tells me.

I don't put it together then, but I do later: all the nights when he came home late "from work" and she screamed at him. We thought he was working hard for us and hated her for it. He looked so defeated, so beaten up. Who knew his silence was that of the culpable?

And much later I remember, through more mature eyes, when I am nine and she is angry at my father and tells me she is leaving him and taking her children back to "her home" in England. He's outside gardening, and I run from the house. I'm sobbing, grabbing at his waist, hugging him hard, and he assures me she won't take us away. But even to a nine-year-old he seems curiously detached, not concerned, considering her wrath.

He knows then what we do not: that she is completely dependent upon him. She has no education, no job skills, and she is worn out from raising four children. She has nowhere to go.

He can continue to garden, knowing the storm will pass. Unlike us, he knows what she's angry about: another woman. But we don't know, and he benefits. We think she's being unreasonable. Crazy! How can she want to leave, after everything he has given her? We have a nice home in a suburban neighborhood and a car. I know from the letters from her siblings that they don't enjoy the luxuries of a backyard or central heating—never mind a new home.

For weeks, I'm terrified to fall asleep, in case she somehow takes us from our beds and we wake up in England, wherever that is.

In later years, she makes him retire from his job early to tend to her, despite the considerable financial strain it puts on them. She's become agoraphobic. He is her sole support, her sole contact in the world outside of television and gossip magazines. (I will think later that she suffers from Stockholm syndrome: the man she blames for capturing her and taking her away from her family, locking her up with four kids in a country where she knows no one, is the only one she wants to see.)

Before she is incapacitated in a care facility, she fends off our visits to their home by having him call us whenever we plan to come by. "Your mother isn't feeling well today. Better not come." We're like Charlie Brown with the football: we know it will be pulled away, but we keep trying.

We think she is his jailor, and we spend decades of emotional energy on the wrongness of it, plotting ways to get him out of the house to our parties and dinners, even if she will not come, but he mostly sticks with her. We don't know that he considers it easier to give in, rather than deal with something, anything, and that this weakness has motivated his actions his entire life.

Then, one day, she has a stroke. She loses her ability to walk, and after a year in hospital, where she refuses even to try the exercises assigned by the physiotherapist, she ends up in a nursing home, where her mind withers away faster than her limbs, as does something she spent her whole life keeping up: appearances.

For all her lack of education, this is a horror. She is street-smart, funny, proud, empathetic to others and, if not in a fury, to her children, too.

She had a sense of humor. She laughed. She was a drop-dead beauty. She could kick her leg up over her head when she danced the tango. She'd put on an Al Jolson or a Broadway musical LP and dance across the living room floor, showing off the woman she once was: a gorgeous redhead with a sense of life and the seductive fecundity of a big-bosomed British babe.

How hard it is to marry those images with others of anger and aggression, never mind the "thing" she has now become. We watch her go from her face lighting up when she sees us—though she can't speak anymore—to looking frightened because she senses she knows us, but doesn't recognize us, to looking as blankly at us as a cow in a pasture chewing cud.

My dad visits her every day for up to ten hours. We think he's a saint. I'm in another city, and I beg him to get a life away from her, to visit her for an hour, but not live in this nursing home that smells of piss and where halls resonate from breakfast through dinner with the moans and screams of the demented.

He insists he is doing what is right, and he talks incessantly about what she eats, whether she has had a bowel movement that day or not and, admiringly, of the other husbands who visit their wives and stay with them all day. He wants to be the loyal husband.

A tad late, I think, many years later.

I make some suggestions.

It starts with card nights with a club, where he runs into his brother and sister-in-law and begins a relationship with the same relatives my mother refused to let him see.

Not, I realize years later, that he had to give in.

They are completely forgiving and delighted and open their arms to him.

Then he reunites with his RAF squadron at first marches on Remembrance Day, then at their dances.

And he begins to attend other dances.

I'm thrilled for him. It's like the old days, before she stopped going out with him.

I remember my youth, and there he is dressed up on a Saturday night. All day long we feel the storm brewing between them. But he will continue on, hopeful that she will once again put on her gorgeous party dress and heels, doll herself up, and go out with him for an evening of tangos and fox-trots.

They are amazing when they dance together, and he is never happier than when he's out socializing with her—the other her—and showing her off. She is a beauty.

But she doesn't get dressed. She's too tired to go out. And finally, as he's pacing in his suit, ever hopeful, she lashes out and screams: he's pressuring her! Deflated, he takes off his suit, and resigns himself to another night of TV. And we are devastated for him.

Now, with my mother confined to a bed and unaware of a world outside her room, I'm so happy he can at last go out and dance again.

Then he meets his lady.

He visits me in Ottawa for a weekend, and before coming he phones to ask if he can bring his "girlfriend."

I think he is kidding.

When I realize he's not, I want to say yes. I don't want to deny this man who has lived so much of his life in a cave; I don't want him to be unhappy. But this is so out of the blue: I didn't even know he was dating. I don't know this woman. I don't know how I will feel about my dad sleeping with someone else in my home. I feel like the parent, not wanting their teenage kids to have sex in their home. So I ask if we can talk and catch up when he's here and if he can bring her next time.

Later, I will regret it: there is no next time.

But we do talk. He has erection problems. She has to "give him a hand." It's pre-Viagra, and he's investigating something archaic that can "pump" him up, literally, so he can make love to her.

Too much information, except for this part, which I'm happy about: he's in love.

He still visits my mother every day—this wonderful woman he's seeing makes sure of that.

She is respectful of my mother, his wife.

And best of all, he has her, he has a life, and his friend is full of life and love for him.

But my sister, Elaine, isn't happy with this. She thinks my dad is betraying my mother and his marriage. So she calls a meeting with the staff psychiatrist at the nursing home. I drive in from Ottawa. My three siblings sit on a sofa together, my dad in a chair off to the side, almost out of their line of vision, and I am in a chair on the other side. My sister lays out the reason for the meeting: my dad shouldn't be seeing this Other Woman.

The psychiatrist puts an end to this notion with a brush-stroke: our mother is so mentally incapacitated at this point, she has no idea whether my father is even visiting her. There is no reason he can't enjoy life.

I'm relieved: Elaine's been at war with my older brother and me for too long over our belief that our father can still visit my mother *and* have a life.

Regardless, he doesn't change her mind. Over the next years, Elaine refuses to allow this woman to come to any family dinners, making my father choose between us and her on Christmas Eve and Christmas Day.

That is a sad outcome. But there is a brilliant one that eventually changes my life. The psychiatrist does something astonishing: he turns on my father—the same man to whom he's just given this support for a richer life—and asks him a question so simple that we are stunned. He asks, "Why?" Why did he do the bidding of a woman who was so clearly troubled? Why did he beat his children at her command? How could he have done this to those entrusted to his care?

Where this doctor's information comes from, I don't know, but this is the first time any of us has heard the suggestion that my father had a choice. With one word, I realize he wasn't a man obliged to follow her bidding, but chose to hurt his children so that he could live in peace. He sacrificed us—with beatings and, in later years, acquiescing to her demand for solitude, including thwarting the visits of his own children—to stop her from arguing with him.

I'm thunderstruck. The man we thought of as our savior—he seemed so balanced, she so off the rails—is actually the guard at the concentration camp, the guy who pulls the trigger because he is told to, the guy who has no responsibility for the scars his children will bear, scars that insecure and abused children bear throughout their lives.

My father doesn't answer. We all wait. We sit silently. The psychiatrist presses him again. No answer.

Now I am silently screaming for an answer.

But that's it. The session is over.

Over the next few years, I try to figure out how to approach my father with this question. I can't believe I haven't thought about it from this perspective.

What happened has affected all of us profoundly, but not in the psychobabble ways some psychiatrists warn of with their damaging—to the damaged—talk of unbreakable cycles.

We're not violent because our mother was. My younger brother is a mother hen to his children, a dad who sacrifices everything for their well-being. My sister would do anything for her kids and, later, her grandchildren. My older brother showers love and presents on his nephews and nieces, and on the children of the women he loves.

For my part, my career will be propelled by the sense of right and wrong and the injustice I've lived through. I feel so responsible for my students at a university where I teach that I meticulously create a plan to protect them, should our class-room ever be invaded by a shooter. I mentor young women who work with me. I launch a charity for girls around the world to help them get an education. Though I'm never blessed with any of my own, I focus on protecting children. I build relationships of love with my nephews and nieces and later choose a husband who has two bright, engaging young children from a previous marriage. When people ask if I'm taking on too much in this relationship, I'm astonished: I am blessed!

It's a long time before I realize that maybe this focus on children is actually a *gift* derived from my experiences as a child.

I begin to wonder how anyone could sacrifice their children for anything. It eats at me. I fight with my older brother about it years after my father dies. He is describing how horrible our mother was: he still sees our dad as the victim, not the perpetuator and enabler.

My father, I realize, is one of those guys everyone in the office likes. He's funny, social, bright. But he doesn't have that core of inner strength that says: stand up and fight for what you believe in.

Stand up and fight for your children.

Deal with your wife so she feels loved, not trapped.

Don't let her take it out on your kids.

And for heaven's sake, don't deliver the blows on her behalf.

He's a courier. A flower delivery boy. A schmuck.

A weakling.

But he's my father, and there is a blood bond, and all my life, until I can figure it out as an adult, he's the one in the house who was fun, and whom I thought loved us the most.

So I'm standing beside his coffin, and I lean over, hug him, and cry. He's not the invincible guy wielding a belt. He's a man with weaknesses, flaws, and a sense of preservation that, sadly, outweighed his obligation to his children.

He's human.

And he loved us.

Of that much I'm sure, all these decades later.

I straighten up and look down to see that I've left a blotch of mascara on his white shirt.

My sweet older brother comes into the room and puts his arm around me. We look down at our father, who looks like he is having a good Saturday sleep-in and could be awakened any moment, and Brent says, "Should I get the ice-cold face-cloth, or should you?"

We scream with laughter, and our siblings come in, completely bewildered. And we are, for that moment, one happy family.

BABY BLUES

— Jenny Rough —

When I saw my baby on a sonogram screen for the first time, the image reminded me of looking at the planet Saturn through a small telescope: a grainy round oval with a dark ring that circled its center, floating in a black abyss.

"It's measuring at eight-and-a-half weeks," the doctor said. It should have been measuring closer to ten.

Sitting there, I remembered the day the pregnancy test was positive. I'd called the doctor, a bubble of excitement in my voice. But her office wasn't able to schedule me for an appointment until the end of the month, even when I begged to be seen earlier.

"December twenty-ninth is the best I can do," the receptionist said.

"But I'm pregnant."

"Nothing much happens in the first few weeks."

This was my first baby. Everything was happening. My body had changed overnight. An extra layer of fat suddenly circled my abdomen. My breasts were bigger. Even so early in my pregnancy, only four weeks along, the embryo was elongating, giving its first hint at human shape. It was busy developing delicate organs. A spinal cord. A heart. Didn't I need prenatal vitamins for that? Ron and I were going to be parents.

The priorities of our lives had shifted in an instant. Didn't we need doctorly advice?

By the time I arrived for my appointment, I was seven weeks and one day into my pregnancy. The embryo was on the verge of becoming a fetus. Our baby's face was taking shape, developing nostrils and eyes. He or she had two little paddles for arms. A nurse drew blood to test my hCG levels (known as "the pregnancy hormone"). High levels are usually a good indicator of a pregnancy that's progressing normally.

When the doctor came into the room, she listened to my list of symptoms and confirmed that these were more good signs. I had morning sickness. Tender breasts. Frequent urination. Sleepiness. An enlarged uterus.

"Any food aversions?"

"Not really."

"You will. I couldn't eat lettuce," she said.

I was dressed in a gown. The doctor ordered me to lie down for a Pap smear. I did what I was told. I had just had a Pap smear in the spring, right before Ron and I left Los Angeles to move across the country so he could take a different job. But this was a new doctor in a new city. I was a new patient. She held an empty folder, a new file.

Back then, I didn't know that the only reason for a Pap smear is to check for abnormal cells on the cervix. I thought maybe there was another purpose—maybe Pap smears were routine for pregnant women who are seven weeks along and having their first prenatal visit. I didn't know that a new doctor in a new city holding a new file is going to automatically order a Pap smear because the doctor doesn't know the patient's history.

She could've asked.

She could've said, "When was your last Pap smear?"

I would've said, "April."

She could've said, "Can you send the results?"

I would've said, "Yes."

She also didn't ask how long it had taken me to conceive. A year and a half. A big red flag. I didn't think to tell her. I believed our difficulties were over. Maybe the doctor would have taken more precautions to preserve our baby if we had talked a bit. If I had known better, I would have taken precautions, too. Instead, the doctor poked and scratched around inside me with a long skinny instrument.

"There's blood," I said after the exam.

The doctor snapped off her gloves. "Lots of women bleed after Pap smears," she said. And she left the room.

The books and experts all say Pap smears don't cause miscarriages. Maybe they are right. Maybe the scraping of my cervix had nothing to do with the fact that my developing child died inside my body. All I know is this: my hCG levels were soaring before the exam (as the blood test later confirmed). After the exam, I was bleeding, and the bleeding never stopped. A few weeks later, the bleeding got worse, and I went for an ultrasound exam. I cried when the doctor told me my baby was dead. I cried again during the car ride home. I cried at the dinner table as I pushed food around my plate, and I cried on the phone with my mom when I croaked, "I lost the baby," before I had to hang up because I couldn't speak another word.

I was paralyzed by the thought of a D&C, but miscarried

naturally within days. First the bleeding turned dark and heavy, then my contractions started.

I called the doctor's office about my labor pains, and I was relieved the doctor on call turned out to be someone other than the woman I'd seen for my appointment. The new doctor was male, and he listened patiently as I explained my predicament through gritted teeth. He informed me that by the time I made my way to the emergency room, the miscarriage would be over. So I collapsed on the bathroom floor, my whole body in pain and discomfort, as Ron sat on the edge of our bed scribbling down the length of time between my contractions: 11:04 PM, 11:09 PM, 11:13 PM. I turned my face aside when the sac dropped in the toilet. Afterward, I crawled into bed, and Ron rubbed my back as I wept.

In the aftermath of my miscarriage, comments by friends and family, although well meaning, didn't ease my pain or grief either, let alone make me laugh. Mostly, they made me angry, teary, and frustrated:

Friend #1: "Get pregnant with another baby as soon as your doctor clears it—even beforehand, if you think your body can handle it."

My inner monologue: I don't want another baby; I want the one I lost.

Friend #2: "Your baby probably had a chromosomal abnormality. It was for the best."

My inner monologue: The fact there may have been complications floods me with even more love for the little guy or girl. I'm full of sorrow that I couldn't protect my struggling child.

Friend #3: "I had a miscarriage, but then went on to have two healthy children. It'll happen to you, too—you'll see."

My inner monologue: It took us so long to conceive this child, and now my doctor is telling me I have endometriosis and he has to remove one of my ovaries, maybe both.

Once, in a surge of bereaved emotion, I wrote a poem about the day Ron and I searched the sonogram screen for a flicker of life, only to discover there was no heartbeat. It was the loudest silence I had ever heard. I also spent hours writing in my journal. All the thoughts, questions, fears, and confusion clattering around in my head needed an outlet. Some entries were furious. Some were sweet. None was funny.

There were days that winter—too many days—when Ron would come home from work at 6 PM to find me under the covers. I told him I had gotten ready for bed early, but I suspect he knew I had been there all day. Despite being in on my secret, he never rushed me through my grief. He was hurting, too, and he would simply come home, set his briefcase on the floor, and rest on the edge of the bed so he could rub my back again.

Eventually, I migrated to the couch downstairs and began working, if only in fits and starts. In February, an editor called with a travel writing assignment. She wanted to send me to Mexico. Ron and I both thought the warm sun and ocean breeze would lift my spirits.

In the warm Mexican mornings, I wandered along the white sand beaches, soft as baby powder, and let the waves lap my feet. In the evenings, I'd return to the beach to sit alone in the darkness. The stars illuminated the night sky, and I wondered about my child. Did he or she have a soul? Did the soul live on?

Three years later, I still wasn't over my miscarriage. My prolonged grief probably had something to do with my inability to conceive again. Month after month, as Ron and I tried for another baby, my empty womb only served as a reminder of the child we had lost. We were neck deep in ovulation kits, herbal concoctions, and medical consultations, trying to figure out the magic combination that would lead to another pregnancy.

In the midst of infertility treatments—the poking and prodding of my private parts, the roller-coaster of emotions, the sadness I would sometimes catch in my husband's face when we visited friends with young families—I stumbled upon an essay by writer Wendy Miller. She had written a humorous story about her three miscarriages. At first the idea offended me, but when I moved my mouse to close the window, the first sentence caught my eye.

I began reading, "Having a miscarriage isn't all bad. Last time I had one my gynecologist validated my parking. Shut up, it's like twenty bucks to park at the hospital, and she never validates. Plus I got a bunch of Darvocet."

A loud "Ha-ha-ha!" escaped, and I immediately clamped my hand over my mouth and looked around. I was home alone, but I was mortified. How dare Miller joke about such tragedy—even her own? And how dare I laugh? The death of a baby in the womb plus *humor*? Those two topics simply don't mix. Yet the first sentence had piqued my interest. I took a deep breath before reading on.

Miller filled an entire page as she yammered on in an amusing way about her three losses.

It felt good to laugh. I had never cracked a smile over my miscarriage, or any of the infertility struggles that followed. But that day, I wondered if laughing about it could help me cope. At least a little?

The day I found Miller's essay, my eyes were glued to my computer screen. I read the entire piece over and over. I was hooked. Miller's essay opened up a whole new world. It takes a lot to make me, a super-serious person, laugh. And Miller had not only found a way to reach my funny bone, but she did so in an area of my personal life I considered off-limits to any jokes, wisecracks, or shenanigans. I cracked up when she wrote, "I'm being sent to genetic counseling. Genetic counseling? Like my DNA could actually change. I think in order for my DNA to change, it has to want to change." For a moment, her comic perspective took the sting out of miscarriage.

I wrote an article about my new discovery—miscarriage humor—for Babble.com. The *New York Times Motherlode* blog picked up my article, and that's when the comments started rolling in. Suddenly, I was immersed in miscarriage humor (and its sister topic, infertility humor) from readers who wanted to share their own funny stories or send me links to irreverent blogs and amusing cartoons on the subject. It made me speculate about how many women were out there—stuck in waves of grief—searching for a path, a road, anything to bring them out of their darkness.

For the longest time I hadn't wanted to associate with other women going through similar struggles. I wasn't in the mood to sit around and wallow even more. But with the flurry of good-humored tales, I realized other women could offer positive encouragement. Maybe talking about miscarriage openly would help me. I heard about a national infertility association called RESOLVE that offers support groups throughout the country. The group in Northern Virginia met at La Madeleine French Bakery in McLean. I sat with six women around the table and listened as they took turns sharing their story. Some women broke down crying at the end of their tale; some began after a few sentences; some would suck in a deep breath, and the tears would start rolling before they'd even uttered a single word. It took a lot of patience to sit through that meeting—and a lot of La Madeleine's napkins. I survived my turn without crying, but I worried my suspicions had been right—maybe a support group would be too depressing.

After practically everyone had burst into tears, our group leader Jane said, "Humor has helped me deal with infertility trials."

All of us paused, and the group's sniffles dwindled into silence as our eyes fell on Jane.

There it was: humor, again.

"It's true," she said. "I memorized a comedy routine. Each time I felt myself losing control of my emotions, like at my best friend's baby shower, I'd recite it. I went from stifling tears to stifling a laugh."

Jane tossed out the idea of going around the circle so we could all share the stupidest thing another person had ever said to us about our situation. "The exercise makes you recognize how ridiculous life can be, and it will help you get unstuck from the refrain 'I'm so sad; this is awful.'"

We didn't try the assignment that night, but I've always wondered what would have happened if we had. Perhaps I would have learned that much sooner how humor serves as a way to give me perspective—to keep me from growing bitter and resentful. Laughing is not my natural instinct, the way it is for some people, but Jane's point about humor was intriguing: that in hard times, we have to make an effort to seek it out. First Wendy Miller and then Jane. It was truly a revelation to me when I realized that even in a place as dark as where miscarriage takes me, humor might help to lighten me up.

A few months later, my younger brother Greg called. I had been suspecting for quite a while that his wife was pregnant, but when I'd inquired about a potential niece or nephew, my probing questions were shut down. I knew the news was going to break as soon as his wife passed the three-month mark, but I didn't know exactly when that was. By the time Greg called, I had completely forgotten about my suspicions.

"Can you do me a favor?" Greg said. "Check your email and click on the link I sent a few minutes ago. I'm thinking of giving Emily this as a Christmas gift. Do you think she'll like it?"

Odd, I thought. I could hear Emily talking in the background. Why would he be on an Internet shopping spree buying her a present right under her nose?

I brushed aside the niggling awareness that something was off and bounded up the stairs, where I pulled up my Gmail account. I opened Greg's message, and there was an ultrasound image of a baby.

A wrecking ball swung into my gut.

A lump the size of a fist bobbed in my throat.

I squeezed my eyes shut, then opened them again. I couldn't help comparing it to the filmy printout my doctor had given me. Greg's child looked so different in this early image. His baby had a distinct head and body, whereas mine had not, having gotten stuck somewhere along the way and never forming into anything past a small, fuzzy blob.

I felt weak. My hands shook, and I had to muster every last bit of strength to squeak out two words: "Aw. Congratulations."

Downstairs, I filled Ron in on the news. He looked at me, trying to gauge my emotions so he could offer the appropriate response. "Well. That's ... neat?" he said.

"I'm so happy," I wailed. I buried my face in his shirt as he stroked my wet cheeks.

That winter, I took a ski trip to Colorado with my other brother Adam. After a long weekend on the slopes, we were in the car heading back east, and our conversation stumbled upon the topic of Emily's pregnancy.

"How do you feel about that?" Adam asked. "I mean, are you okay with her baby and everything?"

I was touched. Out of all the people in my family, Adam was the only one, other than Ron, who had been brave enough to ask how I was coping.

"I'm fine about it now. I'm genuinely happy for them, and I'm excited to have a niece or nephew."

"Me, too. I just feel bad for you and Ron."

I sighed and leaned my head against the headrest. We still had a five-hour drive down to Santa Fe, and that would be just the first of three legs. The next day, and the one after that would be even longer. But the trip had been worth it. Skiing down steep slopes, through mounds of fresh powder in the Colorado sun. And at the end of the day, a salty margarita at a local hangout. For a moment, I told myself that, if I had been pregnant, I wouldn't have been able to bum around with my brother for a ski vacation. And if I had a baby, I probably wouldn't have been able to afford it. But no matter what I told myself, I knew that I'd trade a weekend skiing—or any type of vacation—and an icy margarita for a baby, any time.

Sitting in that car, wanting to push away the pain of my reality, I thought of Wendy Miller and Jane. I thought about how the past few months had been difficult, as I struggled to accept the fact that I might only be an aunt—never a mother. As these thoughts began to well up, I remembered that there was a way out, if only temporarily.

"Know any comedy routines?" I asked Adam.

My brother's face brightened up, and he veered off the highway and into the parking lot of a Barnes & Noble. "I'll be right back. I'm going to go buy a CD. It's hilarious."

I groaned. I adore my brother, but our humor is so different. I was sure he was in the store rummaging through a pile of some sort of silly *South Park*, *The Simpsons*, or *Family Guy* type of nonsense, full of potty talk and lines about diarrhea.

Adam climbed back into the car.

"I'm not in the mood for fart jokes," I said.

"Trust me. You'll like this," he said.

I examined the plastic case as he slid the CD into the player. Who was this pale white guy with a scruffy beard—this Jim Gaffigan?

Turns out, he's a very funny guy. He has the ability to take mundane events—riding an escalator, eating a waffle—and find the humor in them. He even dipped into some black comedy, like joking about the Old Testament story of Abraham climbing a mountain to sacrifice his son.

Adam and I drove on, munching on cheap gas-station candy, watching the New Mexico sky turn pink, and listening to Jim Gaffigan. I was laughing so hard at times I had to wipe tears from my eyes. The good kind of tears.

In the fall of 1992, my wife, Jill, and I got a call from a close friend of Cleavon Little, telling us that Cleavon had decided to take his hospice care at home. She said that friends would be stopping over through the week and that he had asked for us to be included. The sad news was not a surprise—when I had worked with him in Toronto not nine months before, the cancer had already been taking its toll.

The night we went to his house, there were six or seven other people already there. We gathered in the kitchen, while the nurse was upstairs preparing Cleavon to hold court in his bedroom. I remember mentioning to Jill that these other friends were much more intimately connected to him than we were, but she reminded me that we had known him almost the entire span of our acting careers, starting when he and Jill did a Broadway play together in 1974. It was the rollicking comedy *All over Town* by Murray Schisgal. Cleavon was the star, and he was great at keeping the laughter rolling.

Jill tells the story of a performance when one of the actors went up on his lines, and Cleavon tried to help by giving him the cue again. When that had no effect, Cleavon actually tried saying the actor's line for him. But that didn't help either—the poor guy was lost; his eyeballs looked like little bull's-eyes and the flop-sweat was rolling. So, Cleavon casually strolled off stage, found the prompter's script, brought it back out onto the stage, and handed it to him.

"There you go, son. Just read it—nice and slow." And he gave him that look that he was famous for—kind of judgmental and wary at the same time, as if to say, "Whoa, this boy's so slow he's *dangerous.*"

The audience, of course, was having a grand time.

Eight years later, I had my first acting experience with Cleavon in *Two Fish in the Sky*, produced by the venerable Phoenix Theatre. It was a disaster of historic proportion—historic in that the Phoenix, a New York cultural institution since 1953, was plunged ignominiously into the ashes by our production, never to rise again. Cleavon played a London-based Jamaican flim-flam artist with an accent that, despite all his hard work, was completely unintelligible. Added to that was my character, a rabbi who spoke in a pronounced London-Jewish dialect.

The scene between the two of us was like listening to the United Nations on the day the simultaneous translators went on the fritz. We could see the people in the audience shrugging and looking at each other, as if to say "What's going on? Do you understand any of this?" Cleavon, as I recall, remained blithely above the fray, never letting the audience's confusion affect in any way his ebullient good time.

He was irrepressible. From his New York debut in the political satire *Macbird* to his Tony Award–winning performance in the musical *Purlie* to his unforgettable portrayal of

Sheriff Bart in Mel Brooks's *Blazing Saddles,* you could always count on Cleavon Little to light up the moment.

The nurse came down to the kitchen and announced that he was ready to receive visitors. We filed silently up the stairs. Most of the other friends had been around all week; we were the newbies. Jill and I pulled up chairs, while a few of his closer friends sat on the edge of the bed. Cleavon looked like Gandhi: his hair was gone and his body emaciated. He was hooked up to a morphine drip, but the effort it took to move his body made it obvious he was still in a lot of pain. He was at the end of his struggle.

"Well," he said in a small crackly voice, "look at you two little cuties." We were, as I recall, the only white people in the room. "You come to say goodbye?"

We nodded, and Jill went over and kissed him on the cheek.

"If I knew there was a kiss in it, I would have done this years ago."

We all laughed. He started to say something else, but he didn't have much breath. He looked at the man sitting closest to him on the bed and reached his hand out to him. I recognized him as an actor we'd seen years before in New York, but I can't for the life of me remember his name. I wish I could, because his face and his presence will be with me forever.

"Tell them about the show they missed last night," Cleavon said to him.

All the friends chuckled quietly, and Jill and I waited, not knowing what kind of show he was talking about.

"Well," said the friend, and he smiled and shook his head. "Last night, Cleave told us he was ready to die."

"Yes, he was," said a woman who was standing next to the nurse.

"I mean, he'd been suffering this damn cancer long enough, and he knew it was his time, and he had made his peace."

"Amen," said someone softly.

"Yeah, I made the best deal I could get, I suppose," said Cleavon in his crackly voice.

"He said goodbye to each one of us, and we hugged him and kissed him and told him how much we loved him. We were all sitting around on the bed by then. And he said that he was going to close his eyes and let the Lord take him, and we all nodded."

Cleavon closed his eyes as the story was rolling out, so as to give us the proper visual.

"So, his eyes were closed and we each did our individual thing. Some of us, I know, were praying."

"And some of us were crying," said the woman standing beside the nurse. "As quiet as we could be."

"It went on for a long time," said the actor. "I mean, a real long time. Hours, it seemed. None of us wanted to say anything or do anything, 'cause we didn't want to break the spell, y'know?"

"I kept peeking over at the nurse," said another friend, "but she just shook her head. 'Not yet,' she was saying."

The nurse nodded, confirming this part of the story.

"And just when I thought I would burst from all the tension and the quiet and the waiting, I saw this one big eye pop open. Just one. You know, that hairy eyeball thing that Cleavon likes to do, all suspicious and surprised and scared, all at the same time? Like he's saying, 'What you doin', boy?'"

"And this big old eye flicked to the right and then it flicked to the left and it took us all in, one at a time. I was the first to go. I couldn't help myself. I started laughing so hard I couldn't breathe, I swear to God. Then everybody went. The nurse, Cleavon, everybody. It came in waves. We couldn't stop it for the life of us. And in between the waves, we tried to catch our breath and hold our aching sides. And then it came again. I can't tell you how long we laughed."

Two nights later, Cleavon passed, leaving all of us with the memory of his bringing down the house one last time.

INTO THE LIGHT

— *Barbara Lodge* —

My father died first.

When he tripped and fell in a parking lot, I figured he needed new shoes, so we got black Reeboks with extra tread. He wore them to work daily with his gray pinstriped suits, white button-down shirts, and black knit ties. "Trendsetting," he would say, "stylish *and* comfortable." He proceeded to buy them by the dozens to give to friends and family.

Two months later, while wearing his new black Reeboks with that extra tread, he fell again. This time, he suffered lacerations on his face, warranting dozens of stitches.

Several doctors' appointments later, he was diagnosed with ALS, Lou Gehrig's disease. There was no cure. Victims usually die of respiratory failure within two years. Paralyzed. Unable to eat, speak, or move.

Soon after his diagnosis, he invited me to breakfast; I loved having breakfast with my father. We sat on the same metal chairs with the same lemon needlepoint pillows, at the same Formica table, in the same sunny yellow breakfast room where we had eaten my entire life. It was a Saturday morning, my mother was out playing bridge at the club, and he was wearing his navy wool robe, flannel pajamas, and leather slippers. On this day, this usually dapper man looked disheveled. As we ate our eggs, he said, "I've been thinking: my work here is done." I had to breathe and stay steady and calm, so I took his hand. Muscle spasms bumped up under his skin; tiny electric shocks signaling nothing good. His nerves were firing at random intervals, similar to the engine of a car sputtering before it wears out.

He'd made up his mind.

"Where I'm going is a happy place," he said.

"No," I said. "It's not time. You're only eighty-three!"

He assured me he was unafraid and that his mother would be waiting for him.

When he was forty-five, he was pronounced dead during surgery. He described the blinding white light and his deceased mother standing in front of it, her loving arms outstretched.

I had to believe him.

My father was the exhale to my inhale and taught me that anything, *anything*, was possible. So, before this disease stole his body and left his brilliant mind trapped in a paralyzed shell, he was going to move on. I had no say.

For weeks after our breakfast date, he'd sit in his big black leather chair, eyes closed, emptying his mind. Whenever I'd blow into the room, hoping to regale him with stories of my children, he'd respond, "Shhh, silence is okay, too." So I'd sit next to him, holding his hand, already feeling the loss of my father.

"Tomorrow will be the big day," he announced to me and my mother, exactly two weeks after revealing his plan.

My mother was appalled and would have "none of this ridiculousness!" She stormed out of the room and called all three of his treating physicians (who'd become personal friends), asking them to come over, which they did that afternoon. When the cardiologist, internist, and neurologist completed their batteries of tests, including a mobile EKG, their joint conclusion was, "You're not going anywhere anytime soon." As he left the bedroom, one doctor said, "I'm going to see my sick patients now." My mother walked them to the door, wearing her patented "I told you so" grin.

My father winked at me.

Late that evening, he told me to go to Tower Records right away and buy a Barbra Streisand CD containing the song "Memories." I didn't understand his urgency, but had faith he knew what he was doing. I gathered my purse and made for the door.

"Stop! You are going nowhere of the sort!" my mother snapped. "Don't you know the kind of people who go to Tower Records on the Sunset Strip at this hour?"

I ignored her reproach. Apparently, *I* was the kind of person who did just that. My father's body was about to give birth to his soul.

When I returned with the CD, my mother was fuming in the other room, and my dad was still very much alive, serene and comfortable in bed, wearing his yellow flannel pajamas. Without speaking, we played and replayed the song "Memories" so many times we could hear it, whether it was playing or not.

This was his exit music.

He lay on his back with his eyes closed, me curled up next to him, hoping he'd both succeed and fail. When his breathing became almost imperceptible, after several dozen run-throughs of the song, I leaned over closer and whispered, "Are you dead yet, Daddy?" He opened one eye, looked around the room, and said, "No."

We exploded into hysterics, our laughter cutting through all things death and dying and returning us to the simplest form of one another. We held hands and laughed off and on for hours. At two in the morning, he pressed me to go home to my sleeping children. I didn't want to but acquiesced, only after he promised not to stop his heart until I'd finished carpool.

He started manifesting his plan the next morning, as I was dropping off my kids at school. I sensed the shift and sped to his bedside. While holding him in my arms, I felt a rush of energy sweep out of his body, and I knew we would never *ever* be separated. Death may have ended his life, but it didn't end our relationship. For days, even weeks after his passing, I saw and felt miraculous life-affirming energy in all aspects of nature. My father had taken residency in the gentle breeze that rustled the pine trees, and in the pink and orange clouds that streaked across the sunset sky. He was nowhere and everywhere. He was home.

My therapist suggested that such experiences of mystical wonderment, even ecstasy, were nothing more than dissociative denial that my father was actually gone. He said, "You haven't grieved his death and are trying to ignore the emptiness of your loss." I fired him before I even had a chance to go to the cemetery and tell my dad.

I was good at this death thing and considered it my newly awakened life's mission to shepherd dying loved ones into the light. Whether they were open to the possibility or not, I was going to help. Nancy Davenport and I became friends the day I saw her fall off the curb into the gutter. I wrapped my arms around her, lifted her back up to standing, and then introduced myself, recognizing her from my UCLA writing class. The crumpling motion her legs made when she fell reminded me of something all too familiar.

After a few weeks in class, she mentioned she'd been to a doctor because of weakness and difficulty swallowing.

Three weeks later she announced her diagnosis: "I have a disease called ALS."

Instead of feeling averse to being around another victim of the cruelest disease I'd ever known, I drew in closer, invited her to lunches or dinners, and offered to have "writing days" outside of class. I was determined to work my way into her life and begin my tenure as fearless shepherd into the light. The essays she read in class were smart, eloquent, and insightful, a sign she might be open to the idea.

As it turned out, Nancy, a stubborn card-carrying atheist, wasn't. Death was death was death. Death offered no white light, no angels, no waiting family members, no envelopment in universal love. No nothing. Despite or because of that complication, my resolve to help her was unwavering. She was terrified of dying, and I didn't want to be. I mean, I didn't want *her* to be. We spent as much time together as possible.

I gave her a picture of my dad taken a few years before, as he was skipping down a cobblestone street. He'd been waving his arms like wings, and the photo captured the precise moment when neither of his feet touched the ground. His smile was wide and real and free. Unadulterated joy of the sort found in heaven.

Nancy loved the picture and asked me to station it on the coffee table directly in her line of vision. We included him in our conversations, and I told her about his life of abundance and hard work, how he built an empire between tennis games, and how once he was diagnosed with ALS his focus shifted upward. I explained that she was going to a happy place and that family members whom she loved would be waiting for her in heaven.

"Now you've gone too far. There's no one up there." She struggled to stand and pushed her walker out of the room.

My certainty was so "entertaining," however, she chose to keep me around as a curiosity.

Nancy's feeding tube days were quickly approaching, and I wanted to provide her with delicious tastes, hoping a happy stomach would lend itself to an open mind. During one of our precious surf 'n' turf dinners at a local restaurant, I approached the concept of death from a scientific angle.

"Listen, Nancy. I want you to understand this. Energy beats our heart."

She brought a bite of lobster dripping with butter to her mouth, "One of the foods I'll miss most is buttery lobster."

"I know, but listen. Since energy beats our heart and since it's a scientific fact that energy never dies—"

"Did your father like lobster, Barbara?"

"Stop interrupting me! No, he didn't. Energy beats our heart and energy never dies. Are you with me?"

My words were rapid-fire urgent. "It logically follows, then, that when our bodies die, the stuff that beats our heart, our energy, our soul, our consciousness, our spirit, lives on in a different form. This is important, Nancy. Death is not the end. Energy never dies. Do you understand?"

I ordered myself a cosmopolitan martini, briefly questioning which one of us I was trying to convince.

"You're wrong," she said, sipping her Grey Goose on the rocks. "No one listens to our prayers. All that's 'out there' is empty darkness."

"Make it a double," I told the waiter.

When she became homebound, feeding-tubed, and unable to care for herself or pay for help, her doctor called the Servants of Mary, nuns from a local convent who ministered to the sick and dying.

My people, I thought.

The first time I met Sister Alicia, her physical appearance stunned me. I'd never met a real nun before, no less one who was over six feet tall and covered head to toe in a bright white habit and coronet. When Sister Alicia's looming presence entered the room, I swear to God, the entire space was bathed in a warm golden light. Sunbeams surrounded her, even at night. Sister Alicia radiated love.

Nancy had lost the ability to speak, swallow, and walk on her own, and her descent into hopelessness matched my own descent into helplessness. Sister Alicia's presence was, indeed, a gift to both of us.

When she arrived every evening, Sister Alicia immediately

cradled Nancy's hands in her own and said a silent prayer, which Nancy admitted was comforting. She would then routinely remove Nancy's slippers, retrieve a bottle of lotion from her traveling bag, and massage her feet with such tender reverence that awe replaced whatever sadness had wrapped around my heart.

One evening, Nancy's computer's new top-of-the-line voice-assistive technology software malfunctioned, and her computer couldn't speak the words she painstakingly typed. Nancy's only hope of communicating was by pen and paper. Her hands failed her, and I couldn't decipher what she needed. The confident swoops and curls of her once perfect penmanship had devolved into thin, shaky chicken-scratch. Our mounting frustration gave way to her angry tears and impossible-to-understand moaning and grunting, and such a scene was definitely not alright with me. Emboldened by the memory of my father and our purifying laughter the night before he died, I tried to lighten things up.

Nothing caused a rise, not even a reenactment of the time her wheelchair caught air bumping down Westwood Boulevard. Next, I opened a book of her original essays and the more I read aloud, the more captivated she became. My confidence grew.

"Yes," I thought, "I *am* good at this."

Sister Alicia was in the kitchen, and I had an idea. I tiptoed into Nancy's bedroom, opened her filing cabinet, and took out the bottle of Grey Goose Vodka we'd hidden months before. In the living room, I pulled it out from under my shirt whispering "Taa daa!"

I didn't have time to ponder exactly what kind of sin I was about to commit, because in my mind I was simply doing my job. Sneaking vodka into a dying woman's feeding tube, with a nun doing dishes in the next room, was bound to lighten things up. I snuggled close to Nancy on the couch and held the open bottle under her nose. Like two Catholic schoolgirls, we got the giggles. Sister Alicia, humming a church hymn, was preoccupied and I had to act fast.

I uncorked Nancy's feeding tube. My hands trembled.

Noticing a sterilized urine testing cup on the coffee table, I grabbed it, opened it, and poured in the equivalent of three shots of holy water. When I saw Sister Alicia emerge from the kitchen, I sloshed the urine collection cup behind my back. Nancy and I tried to stifle our laughter. Instead, we became hysterical, rolling on the couch and gasping for air so desperately that Nancy really did begin to struggle and we had to turn up her oxygen. As I leaned over to reach the machine, clear liquid delight dripping from my hand, a half-full bottle of Grey Goose was revealed behind me. I closed my eyes, hoping that whatever I couldn't see Sister Alicia couldn't see either. Nancy snorted, and Sister Alicia laughed so hard that the wings of her coronet jiggled. In plain sight of God, this loving nun, and our ancestors watching from heaven, I pulled a generous gulp of Grey Goose into the syringe and shot it directly into the feeding tube. Probably a little too fast. But still.

We three, an unlikely congregation, continued crying and laughing, and Nancy was getting tipsy and loose and free without even tasting the stuff. Her clear eyes and wide smile, the rasping sounds of glee (and Goose) coming from her nose, throat, and mouth, and our free-flowing tears affirmed once again that we were inextricably connected to each other . . . and something much greater.

A few weeks later, Nancy was in the hospital and near death, and I was no closer to convincing her that she was headed to heaven. When we were alone in the room, which was most of the time, her ice blue eyes communicated frozen dread. If anything, Nancy seemed *more* afraid of dying than when we started our odyssey toward the light.

Days passed while I carried her impending death in my bones. I could see it, smell it, and hear it in her shallow breathing. I needed backup, so I put the photo of my dad on her bedside table. By then, her eyes had partially closed, leaving mucus-filled cloudy slits, but I believed she knew it was there.

Wedging myself next to her on the hospital bed and stroking her hair, I promised, "You are not alone; you are loved beyond measure." She groaned. "There's nothing to fear, Nancy." She squeezed my hand and didn't let go. "You're moving toward the light, Nancy. Angels, like Sister Alicia, will guide you. Once you're there, my dad's going to take your hand and ask for the first dance."

Nancy slowly tipped her head in the direction of the photo and smiled. A few days later, she died.

Not long after Nancy passed away, my ninety-four-year-old friend Marcy—the woman who had done our cooking, laundry, and babysitting from the time I was two until I got married—began her own journey toward the light. I told myself that another dying loved one provided me with another opportunity to do my life's work. I was tired, though, and maybe a little scared, so I decided to call the Servants of Mary and request their services for her as well.

Mother Superior summarily rejected my pleas, telling me that Marcy was ineligible. I begged. I offered to donate my Land Cruiser in return. I went to their convent, admitted I was Jewish, and prayed for their help. No way. There were too many others in line who were completely alone, and Marcy was not. She had Jocelyn, a live-in caregiver whom I'd hired a year earlier to help with shopping and cleaning. Marcy was a stickler for a spotless home and never wanted to be taken to an assisted-living facility. After her serving my family for thirty years, I figured I owed her those things.

I can't remember a day when Marcy didn't love and tend to me, my cats, and my dogs as if we were her own. She was the most honest person I'd ever known, not hesitating to tell me when I was acting spoiled or being messy. I appreciated her. I loved her. When homegrown chaos ensued, Marcy was always in the next room dusting furniture. Or cleaning windows. Bringing order. Bearing witness.

When she retired at age eighty-five, assisted by a generous parting gift from my father, Marcy settled comfortably into her studio apartment, filling it with new Ethan Allen furniture and covering the walls and tabletops with dozens of framed photographs of me, depicting every milestone from my third birthday through my wedding and my children's births. Every square inch of her floral couch displayed a needlepoint pillow designed from photos of my childhood pets: Fluffy the cat,

Lady the silky terrier, Anastasia the husky. Whenever I entered her apartment, I was warmly greeted by the Ivory soap smell of Marcy and the memories she held for safekeeping.

Marcy was finally able to live a life of complete independence, which she did with great enjoyment. This diminutive rock of a woman took weekly buses to either the Santa Anita racetrack, Hollywood Park, or Del Mar. She loved to watch the horses. In her free time, she'd study the odds, knit a sweater, needlepoint a pet pillow, or do a crossword puzzle with a ferocity matched only by her cleaning and laundry skills.

After Marcy became too unsteady to navigate the city on her own, I'd visit every few weeks, often bringing my kids. Over McDonald's Happy Meals of cheeseburgers, French fries, and diet cokes, with Lifetime movies blaring in the background, we'd pore over the stacks of photos I'd brought, removing the old ones from her corkboard and replacing them with the new. My daughter, Alex, would sit on the floor and lean against Marcy's legs, so Marcy could brush and brush and brush her messy brown hair into smooth flowing strands of golden silk, just as she'd done when I was Alex's age.

The series of ministrokes arrived one afternoon while we were eating Kentucky Fried Chicken. Marcy's head slumped forward, a drop of saliva ran down her chin. More ministrokes followed, finally landing her permanently in the hospital bed. She maintained her weight from drinking Ensure and eating popsicles, ice cream, and the infrequent French fry. She had become prone to singing "OK OK ok ok ok ok OK" in response to virtually any comment I made or question I asked. How are you feeling Marcy? "OK OK ok ok ok ok OK." Do you want to look at pictures or see a movie? "OK OK ok ok ok ok OK." I interpreted her mantra as a constant assurance that she really was *OK,* willing and able to make the move into the next dimension.

Her doctor suggested we contact hospice when she stopped eating and drinking altogether. Marcy was moving in and out of consciousness and, according to hospice, was actively dying of old age. Every day a different hospice volunteer told me she had hours, if not minutes, to live. One of the volunteers checked daily to determine that I had the emergency morphine at the ready. If she experienced any pain or suffering, I was to put it under her tongue. I threw myself into shepherding Marcy, wanting and needing to be there for her.

Days passed. Then more.

Weeks passed. Then a month.

"Marcy? Are you in pain? Do you need morphine?" asked a volunteer, knowing full well its hastening effects.

Her eyes stayed shut, bony fingers stroking the satin edge of her blanket, "No!"

Each hospice volunteer was more surprised than the last to see her still alive. With my prodding, she finally agreed to speak to Solomon, the hospice chaplain. (Marcy never ignored a great deal, and his services were included in the total hospice package.)

Every Friday evening, stretched to the last fiber of my last nerve, I waited for Solomon in the hall, meeting him with tears, frustration, and the question, "How much longer?"

I started wondering if she were related to Giri Bala, the Bengali yogi who had given up eating and drinking and had existed on sunlight alone for fifty-six years. I took home the sunlight lamp I'd given her for Christmas.

The only person who seemed to be benefitting from Marcy's slow, active demise was Jocelyn, to whom I'd given a handsome raise when I thought the end was near.

On no particular Friday, deep into the second month of her "imminent" death, Solomon and I decided to offer Marcy a white light meditation. We were going to create an aura of calm and tranquility to help her relax into her transition and usher her toward the light with a tad more oomph. The three of us joined hands and the energy flowed through us. (Although, looking back, Marcy might have been sleeping.)

Solomon's velvety voice transported us to a beach where vast oceans of love lapped at the shores of our consciousness. The moon shone full and bright, creating a broad shimmering reflection of the path her spirit would take as it floated into the light.

"It's nowwww tiiiime to go toward the lighttt, Marcy," Solomon whispered.

"Yessss, Marcy, you can go toward the lighttttttt," I chimed in. "Your mother is waiting for you. My dad's there too. Go ahead, Marcy, you have nothing to fear." When I added, "Wait. Marcy, do you see any angels?" Solomon frowned, clearly disappointed in my timing. Nevertheless, we drifted on the gentle sea, and I sensed the presence of something infinite, beautiful, and just beyond my capacity to understand.

Marcy smacked her dry lips, and I offered her a sip of water, which, to my surprise, she accepted. Her eyes, now wide open windows to her soul, looked directly at me. "Oh Marcy!

I love you. I'm here," I spoke into her ear, excited that we'd arrived at the pre-death-energy burst. "You're not alone. Just let go and move toward the light."

Marcy turned her head in my direction and stared. And then, with a voice as clear and huge as the starry midnight sky, she said, "*You* go toward the light!" With that, she closed her eyes and sang the most melodic "OK ok ok OK" I'd ever heard.

Solomon smiled, packed his bag, and made for the door, saying, "I'll see you next week."

Jocelyn brought out her rosary and worked it hard.

I kissed Marcy's forehead and went home for the night. Trailing after me was her voice: "See you later, alligator, OK ok ok."

She died the next week, on an afternoon when I'd left her side to take my kids to a movie. Jocelyn said she went quietly. That night, I tossed and turned and cried and wondered what, exactly, I'd been doing for the past two years, and how her transition had gone without me.

Per her instructions, Marcy was cremated. I chose a rosewood urn because it was sturdy and premium, just like she was. I kept the urn in my closet, however, and seeing it peek out from behind my clothes was unsettling. I moved it to the downstairs coat closet, but she deserved better.

One summer afternoon, I took Marcy's remains and drove up the coast to a valley I knew and loved. Although she'd never been there, she would have appreciated the green grass, frolicking horses, orange groves, and long shadows. I hiked up a hill and found the perfect place, where there were no people and the air smelled of orange blossoms.

"Goodbye, Marcy, I love you," I said. "Thank you for taking such good care of me and my pets." I opened the urn and flung its contents off the hill. A sudden wind blew, and Marcy was flung right back at me, her remains sticking on my toenails and leaving a chalky film on my legs. She even got on my teeth. This was not the inseparability I was hoping for.

I used my sweater to wipe Marcy off of me, but created an even creepier mess. And if there was one thing Marcy *hated*, it was a mess. I had to get out of there.

The ashes scrunched between my toes as I cried my way down the steep trail. I couldn't remember feeling more alone.

"Up. Look up," I heard or thought I heard. And when I did look up, I saw what I'd been missing. The mountains were awash with pinks, blues, and purples, and a single beam of sunlight stretched out from behind a hill, spreading across the entire valley of orange groves.

OK OK ok ok ok OK.

CARAWAY SEED CAKE

— *Carrie Kabak* —

Molly is my grandmother. Her hair is tinted mauve, and she wears marble beads from Connemara over cashmere twinsets. At seventy-seven, she's a tiny scrap of a woman, and this bothers her, so you'll rarely see her out of heels made by Clarks or Bally. And you'll never catch her at a wedding, a funeral, or Sunday mass without a toque, which makes up for the extra twelve inches she wishes she had.

The toque she wears for today's occasion is much like an ice cream cone. It's a complication of pleats, folds, and tucks, and calls for no sudden movement. It requires a calculated turn of the head, and a steady step of the foot, because if it fell off, Oona McNally would see it was stuffed to the gills with newspaper.

Oona is as tall as a rod, and as thin as a rail, and she is joining us for Sunday dinner. We're in a room Molly calls the parlor, and Oona is busy admiring this and verifying that. "A bog oak table such as yours, Molly, is a rare commodity indeed," she says.

She runs the flat of her hand over the tablecloth, seeing to any irregularities. "Is it made of linen?" she wants to know.

"It's the purest damask," says Molly, who is busy setting glasses the size of thimbles on a silver tray. "Would ye both like a drop of sherry?"

"Is it a Harvey's Bristol Cream?" asks Oona.

"Of course it is," says Molly. "Take your glass."

We raise the pure Waterford crystal, and they welcome me to Cloonfree and Carrie looks well, says Oona, and isn't she the spitting image of her Aunt Brona?

Molly shakes her head. "She's more like her Aunt Josie."

And so the debate goes on, until they both come to the conclusion there's no resemblance to the Keagans at all. I'm more like my father.

My visits to Ireland are restricted to the vicinity of Cloonfree, because we rarely leave the house. I'm updated on the progress of the latest family feud, and made aware of all the atrocities, and scandals, and indignities involved. Then I must listen to tales from the past that are interwoven with rumor, belief, and suspicion, which have a tendency to meander and digress.

And then there are the visits from the neighbors, and the passersby, and the postmistress, and the bartender, and the priest, and the nun, and they all become a confusion of surnames in the end, but I must be reacquainted with them all. And I must meet new friends, and old friends, and those I missed last time, such as Oona McNally, who hails from Strokestown, only a short walk from Cloonfree.

"Well, it's lovely to have Carrie home," Molly tells her. "I wondered had she forgotten me."

Oona accepts the offer of a second sherry. "*Sláinte,*" she says. Then she frowns. "Do you have a stiff neck, Molly? God, I hate a stiff neck. The pain can be desperate."

"I have no stiff neck," says Molly. Her head and toque

move as one as she turns to face me. "Help me carry in the dinner," she says.

And so we make journeys to and fro, while Molly tells Oona to set out the Royal Doulton, and to mind she doesn't chip any of it in the process.

And as we serve ourselves to roast beef, cabbage, carrots, and potatoes, I'm treated to a conversation heavy with nostalgia and melancholy, which soon evolves into a recollection of who died, and when, and what did they die of? And did they end up buried in Kildollogue or Kilglass? In Tulsk or Tarmonbarry? And whatever happened to the Cadogans, the Breens, or the Brogans? They moved to England, says Molly, and America, and County Antrim, and County Kildare.

And so the discussion goes on, Molly claiming she could place each body that lived and every soul that expired.

"I doubt that," says Oona.

"I can so!" says Molly, with a jut of her chin.

Oona chews on her beef, then swallows, and pauses awhile. "All right, Molly, tell me this. What happened to Alice Duffy?"

My grandmother looks at her sideways. "Alice Duffy?"

"Where did *she* end up?" asks Oona.

"She took herself to Dublin," says Molly, keeping her eyes trained on her dinner plate.

"Is that so?" says Oona.

At this point, I reach for my sherry, and I'm already thinking of second helpings, because this could turn into the sort of performance I've witnessed countless times, when Molly has been caught out. I have a notion Alice Duffy was plucked out of thin air, but Molly won't back down now. She'll spin a tale until she has her audience and herself convinced this woman existed.

"Alice Duffy had eyes as small as black currants," says Molly.

And we'll be treated to details such as this, and if it's raining, we'll feel it, and if Alice is sad, we'll sense it. And if there's music, we'll hear it.

Oona resumes eating and tells Molly she is losing her marbles, so Molly suggests Oona might be suffering the onset of dementia.

"I'll have you know, Molly Keagan," says Oona, "that I'm as sharp as a diamond!"

"Not as sharp as you think," says Molly. "You can't remember Alice Duffy."

My grandmother is a feisty little character. She's inventive, ingenious, and as cunning as a fox. And for a while, all to be heard is the ticking of the clock, and the gurgling of a stomach, and the scraping of a knife, during which time Molly is most likely setting her stage, painting her scenes, and selecting her dialogue.

"Of course, I remember Alice Duffy," says Oona, finally.

"She had ears the size of an elephant," says Molly.

"And legs as big as his trunk," says Oona.

Oona is a wise woman. If she continues to play along, she's in for a treat.

"Was Alice married to a Fergal, maybe?" Oona ventures.

"She was indeed."

"God, I *love* the name *Fergal*," says Oona.

Molly pours gravy over her potatoes and proceeds to

mash them to a pulp before announcing that Alice Duffy was famous for making caraway seed cake.

"Come on, Molly," says Oona, smiling widely now. "Tell us your Alice Duffy story. I know ye have one."

And so the story unfolds, with Molly only pausing here and there for Oona's interruptions, prompts, or interjections. Or to gather a portion of meat on her fork, along with a shred of cabbage, a scoop of potato, and a slice of carrot.

"The bog was damp," she begins, "and deathly quiet."

The turf was piled low like burial mounds, and the sky had a frown on its face, and soon rain would send slanted mists across the lake. Molly and her sister Bridie watched Alice Duffy bend down to pick up yet another sod, and just above her ankle sock they saw a bruise the size of a chicken egg, in shades of blue and yellow and gray.

"Was it the kick of a mule?" asks Oona.

"It was the mark of a man's leather boot," Molly tells her.

It was always Fergal's job to fetch the turf, but he had been missing for seven days by now. Daddy and Uncle Mickey were tending the Duffys' cows, and Mammy and Grandma were seeing to the hens and the geese. Fergal will turn up sooner or later, they said, and no doubt as drunk as a louse.

Alice promised Molly and Bridie a wedge of caraway seed cake if they'd help her fetch the turf. Aw, Jesus, they thought, and if Fergal decides to come home, she'll want to keep us all night.

But Mammy said it would be bad manners to refuse.

Alice's caraway seed cakes were as big as cartwheels. She'd spread great slabs of it with butter and vegetable marrow jam, and when you'd finished an hour later, she'd beg you to stay, because sure, hadn't you only just arrived? And she'd brew yet another pot of black tea, and fetch her knitting, and urge you to keep on talking as she plained one, and purled one, and passed one stitch over, stripe after stripe.

"And sometimes she'd stick a needle up her nose," decides Oona. "To prize out the bogeys."

"Oona McNally," says Molly, "I've never understood why you're so fascinated with dirty habits."

"*Arrah*, shut up," says Oona, "and get on with it."

I nudge my grandmother to urge her to keep going.

Well, Alice's mule did nothing but bray and bellyache because the threat of a storm was scaring the living shite out of him. *Yip*, you ould fecker, said Bridie as she pulled him along. *Yip!*

And then Alice said, Wait a minute, girls, while she squats by this bush, because she'll die if she doesn't pee soon. And when she hoisted her skirts, the sisters were horrified to see her shins were a mess of open sores.

"Sounds like the poor creature had ulcers," says Oona.

"More likely wheals from a man's belt," says Molly.

"Was there a lot of yellow pus?" asks Oona. "Because that's one way of knowing you definitely have ulcers."

"Jesus, Oona," says Molly. "Will ye give over?"

My grandmother pushes the dish of potatoes toward me and hands me the carving knife. "Carrie, help yourself to more beef, and whatever else you want. Don't wait to be asked." She waits for Oona and me to pile our plates again before she takes us back to the bog.

By the time the panniers were full, the rain had turned into a deluge of pitchforks. Alice decided they'd best be on their way, and now she had turf she could boil the kettle for a nice pot of tea, to wash down the caraway seed cake.

She'd ply caraway seed cake on the tinker who stole clothes off the washing lines. She'd urge the postman to try a piece, go on, *do*. She'd suggest he take the weight off his legs for a while. The baker, the tailor, the soldier, the sailor: she'd invite them all in, to pass the time of day. Even the Royal Irish Constabulary, who carried carbines, and handcuffs, and bayonets.

Fergal couldn't land Alice a fat lip if they had company.

And as Molly, Bridie, Alice, and the mule left the bog for drier land, they heard a mournful cry that was laden with anguish, and heartache, and pain, and Alice said they mustn't look over their shoulders at the marsh, in case they saw the Banshee walking there, dressed in her shroud, and wringing her bony hands.

As they trudged through the fields of Cloonfree, the storm subsided. They passed hedges, and strings of trees, and a stretch of brooks. Their clothes were drenched, and the mule farted with every skid of his hoof. But Alice would soon have a fire burning, and she had some dry clothes to spare. They passed the ruins that crumbled under shawls of ivy, and when they finally reached the wall that bordered Alice's cottage, she yelped with excitement, because she spied a little gathering in her yard. She had visitors!

And, what's more, there was plenty of caraway seed cake to go around.

When the picture ahead focused into a clear view, Molly and Bridie saw that it was three men that stood by the old well, and they had a horse harnessed to a cart. Then Alice clapped her hand to her mouth, and lifting her skirts, she galloped the rest of way, through puddles, and mud, and a scatter of hens.

Molly hitched the mule to the gatepost, and as she followed her sister, she clenched her fists, for God save us and bless us—there was a dead body in that cart.

Is it the Banshee, screaming loud and clear
By the old broken tree, I hear, I hear?

"Jesus, Carrie," says Oona, laying down her knife and fork. "Hand me that packet of cigarettes—I need a smoke."

The solemn faces of Father Hegarty, Gyles Pelly, and Sergeant Smyth told Alice it was Fergal lying in that cart.

The priest reached out for Alice, but she shrank away, stopping her ears with the heel of her hands, like she wanted to block out all sounds. Like she didn't want to hear any words.

Sergeant Smyth raised the edge of the blanket, and Molly and Bridie saw a gray toe that was missing a nail, and that's when Alice let out a piercing cry. And then Fergal's body was exposed, to show rags adhering to flesh, and he was bloodless like a pig in a larder, and his eyes, like marbles, stared at the thundercloud above. Sweet Jesus, wasn't a toe enough for them to see? said Bridie. And Alice slipped to the ground, and lay motionless, reduced to a loose heap of shawl, and skirts, and headscarf . . .

"Well!" says Molly. "I think it's time for dessert now."

"For the love of God," says Oona, wiping away a tear. "Will you give us a minute? Now I'm depressed as hell."

Oona strikes a match to light another cigarette, and Molly is riled to see she stubbed the first on the Royal Doulton. So I stack the plates and promise to return from the kitchen with an ashtray. "And I might as well fetch the trifle from the fridge, while I'm at it," says Molly.

The trifle is a flamboyance of custard, cream, and peaches, over sponge fingers doused in cognac, and all is arranged in a glass bowl the size of a basin. It's a sight to see.

So back to the parlor I go and I hand Oona the ashtray, and I set the trifle in the middle of the table, so pretty against the damask tablecloth.

Oona takes a puff of her Woodbine and sizes it up. "The best trifle I ever had was at a wake," she says. "God! Were you at Fergal's wake, Molly?"

"I was. And so would you have been, if ye knew Alice Duffy, like ye said."

I serve the trifle, a scoop each, and I'm careful to include a bit of everything.

"Wait now, wait now," says Oona, tapping her head. "It's all coming back to me."

"Put out your cigarette," says Molly. "You're shaking ash into your trifle."

"Fergal drowned in Lough Ree," says Oona, "and his body swelled like a balloon."

"He drowned, did he?" asks Molly.

Oona looks at her steadily. "Yes. He did."

So Molly tells us to imagine Alice Duffy's cottage, which was built of limestone, and had three rooms, a thatched roof, and a small row of outhouses.

The sisters didn't want to look inside the casket, but Mammy said it was expected. It was called *viewing*. Fergal was on the kitchen table, and Molly wanted to know why there were pennies on his eyes, so Mammy explained it was to keep them closed.

Sure, *he* won't be waking up any time soon, whispered Molly.

Alice asked them if they'd do her a favor and start knocking on doors to beg for the loan of a few candlesticks.

When evening came, people swarmed Alice's kitchen and clogged every corner.

Ohhh, Fergal, sighed Old Mary Godfrey. Why did ye have to drown? And then she howled like a wolf, and Mammy said that was called *keening*.

He was a fine man! cried Old Mary Godfrey. A lovely man! A holy man!

Was he, my arse, said Ethna Fitton.

He must have taken the boat too far out, whispered Kathleen Doody. The middle of Lough Ree is treacherous.

The boat washed up only this morning, said Ethna Fitton, and there were three empty bottles of *potheen* inside.

Dear Mother of God, *no!* said Kathleen Doody. The ould rascal!

Still, said Ethna Fitton, it might be the best way to go, drunk as the *divil* himself.

And all this time, Alice remained in her corner, and Mammy was urging her to take a bite of something, come on now, do, or maybe a little drop of brandy, to give her strength. And Father Hegarty was saying, Now, 'tis well that Fergal went first, Alice. He'll intercede for you in the next world, so he will. And he averted his eyes, knowing full well there'd be no ascending any golden staircase for the likes of Fergal, may God have mercy on his wretched soul.

Kathleen Doody and Old Mary Godfrey sliced Alice's salt ham and handed it around liberally, along with the last of her bread. And they followed up with slices of caraway seed cake, spread with butter and vegetable marrow jam.

"God, Molly, ye'ere great at remembering all those names," says Oona. "I'll give ye that." She leans forward. "What's the betting Fergal had some fancy woman!"

"Fergal wasn't always fishing at the lake," says Molly. "He cast his rod in a few other places, too."

And so we return to Alice Duffy's house.

It was midnight before the Mullan boys trooped in. They expressed their sympathies and shook their heads. Such a tragic, tragic occurrence, Alice, where will we play? Over here, perhaps, away from the door? Instruments were carried over shoulders, or under arms, or in their pockets: the bodhrán, the fiddle, and a tin whistle.

And following close behind, in stepped none other than Fanny Lynch, with her scarlet lips and penciled eyebrows. She had bosoms the size of two barrels and was known for her loose morals and paid favors. And she looked in at Fergal lying there with his clasped hands, and his copper pennies, and she ranted and raved, and sobbed and spluttered, and Father Hegarty was pulling at her saying, Go home now, Fanny Lynch! Go home to yer three children that are left all alone.

Alice Duffy thumped across the kitchen and lunged at Fanny Lynch, and they pinched, and they punched, and they spat, and they squawked, and Gyles Pelly yelled, Stop! For the love of God, stop! Sure, Fergal planned on leaving ye both, anyway!

And he showed them papers he'd found in Fergal's pockets, which he'd had a divil of a job drying out. But Alice couldn't make out the words, because she couldn't read or write.

Read out loud, Gyles Pelly! everyone shouted. And let us see the pictures!

"I have an awful pain in the head," says Molly, touching my arm. "Would ye brew a pot of tea, Carrie?"

"Jesus, Molly," says Oona. "The suspense is killing me. Take off the toque, and ye'll be fine. It must weigh a ton."

"I will not."

"I'll be two minutes," I say, tearing out of the parlor.

I slam the kettle on the Aga, shovel Ashbys Irish Blend into the pot, and slosh milk into a jug. China cups, doily on a tea trolley, sugar in cubes. All presented the way Molly likes it.

Rattle, rattle, rattle into the hallway, past the coat stand, past the grandfather clock, past the picture of the Immaculate Conception, and back into the parlor.

"Here we are," I say.

"Thank God," says Oona. "It took ye till tomorrow to get here. Will I pour? Come on, Molly, what was on those papers?"

Gyles Pelly held them up for everyone to see, like he was the master at a school. There was jostling going on, and shoving, and pushing, but Molly and Bridie managed to edge forward, nevertheless. They saw pictures bordered with a chase of shamrocks, with harps and hills in the background. Irishmen held *shillelaghs*, or played pipes, and women in aprons were asking, "Will you go, or must I?" And one poster said: "An Irish hero! One Irishman defeats ten Germans."

And there was a poem:

What have you done for Ireland?
Have you answered the call?
Have you changed the tweed for the khaki
To serve with the rank and file
As your comrades are gladly serving,
Or isn't it worth your while?

Father Hegarty placed his hand on Alice's shoulder. I'm sorry, he said. Seems Fergal signed up for the Irish Guards only a month ago.

Thank you, Father, said Alice.

She watched Fanny Lynch walk out of the door and into the night. Then Alice turned on her heels, and the crowd divided like the Red Sea before Moses to let her through. But she didn't go back to her stool. She stood next to the Mullan boys instead, and asked them to play "Johnny, I Hardly Knew Ye."

And the pipes were coaxed to cry their tune, and the fiddle rippled faster than a mountain stream, and soon the bodhrán was thumping like a beating heart.

And when they had finished, Alice said, That's enough sadness for now, and she'd like the boys to play something merry the people could dance to.

It wasn't until well after the beer was passed around that anyone took to the floor. Daddy and Uncle Mickey were the first to start because Mammy urged them on. It's what Alice wants to see, she said. The poor creature.

AND one, two, three, they cried, flapping their elbows, and hammering their feet. Men trooped to the floor to join them, and soon Father Hegarty himself, who was well oiled by now, was spinning in circles like a whirling dervish. Molly couldn't see too well over all the bobbing heads, but she was sure she saw Alice tapping her foot.

When the cock crowed, stars blinked in a mauve sky, and it was well time to close the lid on Fergal Duffy by now. And Molly and Bridie ran to the casket, curious as to why they heard gasps, sighs, and a shock of exclamations. *God almighty!*

Would ye take a look at that? Dead as a doorknob Fergal might well have been, but a grin as wide as a tooth comb had taken form on his face.

More like an expression of sheer mockery, according to Alice. And so far, no one had caught even a spark of rage in her eyes. But now they rolled, and her nostrils flared, and her face simmered and came to a boil, and she yelled, *Go n-ithe an cat thú, Fergus Duffy! Is go n-ithe an diabhal an cat!* And then may ye all rot together!

And Alice took it upon herself to holler with joy, for the bastard was dead! And wasn't she as free as a lark now?

It took her long enough to realize that, said Ethan Fitton.

Close the lid, Gyles Pelly! everyone cried. And when the last nail was driven home, Alice called for the Mullans to play a reel, and lines formed, and hands clapped, and an arch of arms spread well into the yard. Alice skipped down the middle, and she twisted and kicked, keeping with the rhythm and the pattern of beats, and in perfect time with those close behind her.

The music came to an end, and Alice stood panting, and wanting more.

It's not right, Old Mary Godfrey muttered. *It's just not right.* First the priest and now the wife. Dear Mother of God, what is the world coming to?

And Alice flung back her head, and laughed, showing an arc of white teeth.

She'll be dancing on his grave tomorrow, sneered Old Mary Godfrey.

"And did she?" asks Oona.

"To this day, her ghost can be seen dancing in the cemetery," says Molly. "But only if there are stars blinking in a mauve sky."

I pour my grandmother a third cup of tea.

A small payment indeed, for such a grand performance.

"What's to be afraid of?" Al says. "I don't remember where I came from, and I'm just going back to the same place." He seems quite cheerful about this.

We're having lunch at the Belmont Brewery, overlooking the beach on a beautiful Southern California day, and he's drinking a beer. Usually we're talking about politics, but today we're discussing death.

"And remember, no funeral. I have it all planned." He takes out his wallet and pulls a card from it. "Neptune Society. They take care of the whole thing. See the number on it? It's a pre-plan."

I look at the card. Frankly, I find it a little creepy. My father did the same thing. He visited the local East Hampton funeral home and had a long discussion with the director about how exactly he wanted them to handle it all when he died.

"And I've paid to have my ashes taken to sea," Al says.

"I'll go on the boat," I say.

"Oh, no, you won't."

"Of course I will. We'll have a service. The whole family." I can envision grandchildren tossing flowers into the water, the grown-ups telling loving and funny anecdotes about Al, perhaps holding flutes of champagne.

"There will be no service." He pats my hand. "I'm Jewish, but not religious."

"We'll call it a memorial."

"No, nothing. Gone is gone. Nobody's going on the boat."

"Maybe I really want to go."

"Nope." He offers me a sip of his beer. "No tubes, remember that. No machines."

Finally I promise, no tubes, no machines, and no memorial at sea.

When my mother first moved into The Breakers, a retirement hotel in Long Beach, California, I read about Al in the hotel newsletter; his wife had just died, and he didn't want any visitors or anyone trying to talk to him. A few weeks later he resurfaced, appearing at meals and, to my utter shock, my mother—a widow who had been married to my father for fifty-five years—was giving him the eye.

"He's attractive, isn't he?" she said as we had lunch one day and he strode into the dining room wearing tennis clothes. He was attractive—he was in his late seventies then, five years younger than she was, tall, lean, and athletic. But this was my mother. She already had another guy courting her that she barely tolerated because he was a Republican and too conservative. Then one day, Al (who turned out to be a liberal Democrat) heard my mother playing the piano—something by Mozart—in the lobby of The Breakers, and next thing I knew they were a couple. "I thought my life was over," he would tell me later. "But there she was, so beautiful and playing the piano!"

Al also played the piano, old tunes from the forties by ear. My mother began to give him piano lessons, teaching him to read music. They took long walks, held hands, laughed a lot, read the paper together every morning, and had martinis together every night. Then a year or so after moving into The Breakers, my mother suddenly decided she was too young to be living in a retirement hotel—my mother, the queen of denial. She was in her mid-eighties and had heart problems, but in spite of myself, I admired her determination as she packed up everything, including her piano, and moved ten miles north into her own apartment in Palos Verdes. Al drove up for lunch a few times a week, and she'd cook elaborate meals for him. Did he spend the night? I wondered but never asked.

She eventually realized she really couldn't live on her own any longer, so a few months later everything got packed up again, and she and her piano returned to The Breakers. This time she moved into an apartment right down the hall from Al. In spite of her health, she practiced the piano constantly (up to six hours a day), gave recitals, and loved her new apartment. This was really the happiest I'd ever seen my mother. She was mellowing in old age. Al adored her. He gave her the diamond rings that had belonged to his wife.

He wanted to marry her, but she thought she was too old to get married again. "Darling," she said to me one night at dinner, "if I were in my seventies, I might consider it, but good God, I'll be ninety in four years." However, she kept advising me to remarry. She wanted my boyfriend for a son-in-law; I wanted hers for a stepfather.

Al's marriage, childless, had been a long and happy one. He and his wife had both worked. He had been in the army and then for years drove a cab in San Francisco, a job he had loved. He also loved to tell stories of those days—being held at gunpoint, the vast array of characters he'd had as fares—and his very favorite story, the time he drove Edward Kennedy to the San Francisco airport. His only living blood relative now was his cousin George, a professor at Berkeley. "The smart one in the family," Al would say, laughing.

My mother's heart got weaker. Then she had to have a walker, and visiting nurses came every morning. When her breathing became difficult, Al would spend the night in the chair next to her bed, watching over her. One day when I arrived and a nurse was there, my mother whispered for me to get Al's diamond rings out of her jewelry box.

When I got them for her, she slipped them on her fingers. "I don't want them to think I'm easy," she said.

"Who?" I asked.

"The nurses—they know he spends the night."

A few months later, when she was dying, Al walked the hospital hallways with me, holding my hand. He was with her when she died one early dawn, just before my brother and I got to the hospital.

My mother had never mentioned death; she could not, would not discuss it. She refused to acknowledge that she would ever die. So there was not only grief that morning, but also confusion. "Now what?" said my brother.

I hadn't a clue; she'd conned us all into thinking she'd live forever. How do you prepare for this? Does everyone, if they haven't been given clear instructions, get caught in the middle of shock, loss, and grief, trying to figure out the practical details? I thought of my father at the funeral home making arrangements, and Al with his prepaid plan—oh, not creepy at all, but thoughtful! But no, not my mother. I was suddenly furious at her. Always in denial, right up to the end.

I told my brother that cremation certainly seemed the simpler, more practical option. Thinking we were going to have to go coffin shopping, he breathed a sigh of relief. We looked up cremation services in the Yellow Pages at the nurse's station, found a company, and went to their nearby office that morning.

The woman in the office annoyed me right off the bat. Her hair was sprayed and teased, she was wearing a suit, and she assumed my brother was in complete charge and directed her entire speech to him. When she got to the part about the "cremains" being ready by the end of the week, I made little humming sounds so I wouldn't break into hysterical hoots of laughter. Her euphemism sounded like something horrible that could go wrong with a damp basement. *Ashes* was such a fine, straightforward word; why couldn't she just say that the fucking *ashes* would be ready to pick up in three days? (How good it felt to be so angry! It filled me up, left no room for grief.)

I thought of my father leaving instructions not only with the funeral home but also for distributing his ashes. "Find someone with a fishing boat, and take my ashes out to sea," he'd told me once as he drank a large bourbon on the rocks and pointed to the ocean—which is exactly what my brother and I did, grateful for such clear directions. It would be eight years before I finally figured out what to do with my mother's cremains.

In the months after my mother's death, I'd visit Al, he'd play the piano for me, and I'd cry. He wouldn't say anything or attempt to make me feel better. He'd just play those old tunes from the forties and let me sit there and cry.

He had become an integral part of my family by then, and when I finally married my boyfriend and my family grew even larger, this man who had never had children of his own now had, in addition to my two daughters and their husbands, my three stepchildren and their spouses and partners. With the arrival of my grandchildren, Al became a great-grandfather. For a decade we visited regularly.

I loved talking to him about my mother; he gave me a side of her I didn't really know. Though sometimes it went beyond what I wanted to know. "She was a passionate woman," he said once. I covered my ears, and he laughed.

When he gave up his car, I'd drive down to see him and we'd have our lunches sitting in the sun overlooking the beach, always at the same restaurant. Eventually he began to grow frail in spite of his vigorous exercise program; he was almost ninety before he gave up biking and using a rowing machine, but his mind stayed sharp and involved in the news and the stock market.

I'd been traveling a lot one summer. When I got home, I called Al to confirm a long-standing lunch date we had, and he sounded distant. He didn't feel up to going out, he told me. I made another date for the following week and he said, "Sure."

"I'll call you and confirm," I said.

"Sure," he repeated.

My feelings were hurt. I thought he'd be happy to have me back. Was I being intrusive? Did he want to be alone?

A few days later, I got a call from the nurse at The Breakers. Al was dizzy and had fallen on the street. His arm was bleeding and he needed to go to the VA hospital. I told her I'd be right down and jumped in my car.

In the month I'd been gone, Al had transformed into a fragile old man, fearful and forgetful. He seemed to recognize me, though, and smiled. I got him in the car, and he asked me where we were going. "The VA hospital," I said. "You're going to see a doctor."

"Good." He gazed out the window. A minute later he asked, "Where are we going?" For the whole drive to the hospital he asked that question over and over, and I'd answer over and over.

To make the hospital paperwork easier, I told the VA that I was his stepdaughter. As we waited to be seen in the emergency room, he began to relax and grow less frightened; he finally realized he was indeed at the hospital. We went in to see the doctor. Though Al had a deep gash on his arm, there were no broken bones, and his sense of humor was still intact. When the doctor asked him how old he was, Al said, "106."

"Stop bragging," I said.

"I'm not 106?" He looked at me, genuinely surprised.

"You're 92," I said, realizing that he really didn't remember how old he was.

"Well, what do you know," he laughed, and then the doctor and I laughed too.

We drove back to The Breakers, Al once again his cheerful self. "Are you sure I'm not 106?" he asked me.

"Positive," I said.

"Well, I sure feel 106."

In the following year he would have times of clarity, but our lunches together changed. His hearing, always bad, became worse. Finally, we had lunches in the dining room of The Breakers instead of at the Belmont Brewery by the beach. Because he was always losing his hearing aids, I'd write him notes: "YOU HAVE A DOCTOR'S APPOINTMENT NEXT WEEK!" "DO YOU NEED A NEW BELT?" "YOU'RE LOSING WEIGHT!" All in caps, like shouted messages. His eyesight was failing, and his glasses were getting to be a problem, too.

I began to find his meticulously kept apartment in disorder—piles of clothes in the living room, plates not picked up. "They just leave my clothes everywhere," Al said. I stormed down to the manager's office to complain. "We try," said the manager. "Al pulls his clothes out of drawers and the closet and dumps them on the floor. He won't let us take the dishes. He's still drinking martinis. We don't know what to do."

And neither did I. I was in constant contact now with his cousin George, sending him Al's mail and bills, and every few months George would fly down to visit him and we'd have dinner. There was talk of whether Al should have a hernia operation; the nurse said his hernia was the worst she had ever seen. But he was getting weaker, too weak for an operation. We called hospice.

Lunches together were now in his room on a tray, and there was no conversation, spoken or written. But I wanted to be there, and I wanted the people at The Breakers and the hospice nurses to know he was loved and had a family. The martinis were still a problem; one night he drank an unknown number of them and went down to the lobby and left The Breakers. He had to be chased down the street.

Months went by. He didn't die, so hospice left.

My husband and I have a trip planned in April: "WE'RE GOING TO FRANCE!" I write on a card. And Al nods. "France!" he says.

Just before we return from our trip, I get an email from George saying that hospice has returned and the nurse just called him to say that Al is close to the end. He's flying down to Long Beach as soon as he can get on a flight.

My husband and I return late that night, and early the next morning I get on the freeway, praying I won't be too late. George is on a flight that arrives early afternoon.

The hospice nurse lets me into his apartment and Al is in bed with his eyes closed, unconscious, but he looks like he's sleeping. The nurse, a new one I don't know, says it's very close to the end, he's probably been waiting for me to return. I hold his hand, all bones and bruised skin, and talk to him.

Can he hear me? I've read that hearing is the last sense to go, so I believe that he does know I'm here.

Sun pours into his little apartment, the radio is playing music, and as I sit next to his bed, I explain to the nurse who everybody is in the family photographs—my mother celebrating New Year's Eve with him, my brother, my husband, our children, and all the grandchildren. I tell her the story of Al and my mother's romance, the piano playing, the handholding. He's no longer her anonymous dying patient; he's a man who has had a wonderful romance in old age with a beautiful woman, a man with a large family who loves him dearly.

Here's something I've never told anyone because it sounds so farfetched, so odd, but it's true: on the radio, Tony Bennett is singing that he left his heart in San Francisco. The soundtrack for Al's death. Can Al hear it? I hope so.

His breathing begins to change and there's a sigh, then silence, and he's gone. In his own bed, with no tubes, no machines.

His wallet is on his dresser. I take out the Neptune card, grateful for his planning to make it easier for us to handle, for not being in denial about dying someday. I call and give Neptune his prepaid number and they say they'll be there in an hour or so. The help at The Breakers—the housekeepers, the cooks, the repairmen who have helped care for Al this past year—all come in to pay their last respects, crying and telling me what a good man he was. His cousin George arrives. The hospice nurse leaves for lunch. George goes to check into his hotel.

I'm alone with Al's body in the apartment. I'm sure he'd have had a fit over this. *Gone is gone.* He'd have told me to leave, go home, this isn't part of the plan. But I don't want to leave him alone.

Finally, the Neptune guys show up, polite and dignified in their shiny black suits, and I hand them Al's prepaid card and go over the paperwork with them. Then they both go into Al's bedroom with their stretcher and I can hear the rustling of the body bag and I remember what Al had said about death and how unafraid he was. It doesn't feel like Al going into that bag, it's like an old suit being collected that he left behind.

And suddenly I realize I can have the real Al again. Not the confused and frightened old man who had dumped piles of clothes on the floor, whose mind became muddled, but the guy my mother fell in love with, who had given her diamond rings and made her happier than she'd ever been, and who loved playing the piano as much as she did. The real Al who has simply gone back to where he came from.

SUBURBAN ANIMATION

— *Joshua Braff* —

The Zenith my parents bought in 1978 had five channels and weighed about as much as an economy sized Buick. It took seven minutes to produce a picture, which began as a Tinkerbell-sized dot in the center of the screen. When school ended each day, I'd tear off for home, pluck the circular on/off button, and make myself an Ellio's frozen pizza, which would be finished a few minutes after Tinkerbell morphed into the Road Runner. The premise of this program was biblical: coyote chases fast bird, but fast bird is more desert-savvy than coyote, so food chain theory gets turned on its head, and hilarity ensues.

In hindsight, I see that I cherished this particular cartoon because I, in fact, was the Road Runner. With no voice whatsoever, save for a "beep-beep" here and there, and using only his remarkable speed and quiet intellect, he outwits his tenacious nemesis and is free to run. No one in my life in 1978 wanted to eat me. But elementary school was my coyote, and I couldn't get away fast enough.

On this particular Tuesday afternoon, the Zenith came to life just as the coyote was plummeting off a cliff and his body was about to smack the earth in a small mushroom cloud of brown smoke. I'd missed the setup as I had tried to cool my pizza and was distracted by the sound of a vacuum cleaner just outside the den. It was Janice, a woman who was once employed as a nurse in her native Haiti, but was now a housecleaner, our babysitter, and an American citizen. I knew she missed the life she once had, and it always made me sad for her. She said that being a nurse gave her "purpose in life," and it was hard for me to look at her and not think about these words.

The vacuum bumped the edges of the wall in a lonely and graceless drone. To and fro, repeat, to and fro, and it drowned out my show, leaving the TV screen snowy with static. I got closer, turned up the volume even louder and began, as I often did, to envy the ease of being animated, the utter freedom to scatter and smash, to chase and fly. BOING! ZOINK! ZOWIE!

I took a bite of my pizza, but it was too soon, way too soon. The cheese slid off, and the sauce underneath was hotter than lava, capable of burning a hole through German steel. *Auuuugh!* The skin was burned off the roof of my mouth, riddled to raw by the magma-hot sauce. I touched it with my tongue, knowing I'd be feeling it all night, and tomorrow in school, while my teacher clicked her chalk against the board in a cloud of endless monotony.

Janice rolled closer, just outside the TV room, and I turned to her because the sound was erasing every zoink! and zowie!, every boink! and doing! I knew she was lost in the task, dreaming of doing anything but running over Cheerios with our vacuum cleaner, and I squeezed my eyes shut to avoid the thought of it. And when I opened them the coyote, who'd strapped himself to a lit missile, was soaring toward the Road Runner with a huge and confident grin. This animal had amazing optimism for someone who failed as often as he did. The vacuum shut off for a second, and the silence was joyous.

BOING! ZOINK! ZOWIE! Yes! But then my younger sister and brother came barreling into the room, chasing each other and toppling near my plate of pizza, blocking the television with their lesser sibling selves. "Move!" I barked, but they didn't listen. My brother, Alex, a toddler, was smothering my little sister, Rachel, and she screamed in his ear and slapped his butt, and I starting watching them like I watched the television, adding to their mayhem by lightly jabbing any bit of flesh that pointed my way. Rachel's foot hit my pizza, and it sprayed sauce on the laces of her white sneaker. "Hey!"

"Whoops."

"Move!" I said again, and they did, to the couch where they settled, quieted, watching the cartoon. The pizza was okay, thank God. Rachel, sucking her thumb, leaned on a huge floor pillow with a barn setting painted on it. The sheep looked like polar bears, and for some reason a zebra was in the yard, eating where the cows should have been. Alex sneezed and had a bubble of snot expanding from his nose. It filled and rounded while he ignored it and laughed at the way the Road Runner pulled to a halt just before a cliff, leaving the coyote to overrun the edge, dropping once again. Alex giggled and looked at me, swiping at his nose with his elbow.

In the quiet, I could hear the wind outside making a swirling, high-pitched whistle, and a tapping began on the window above the TV, as if someone out there were trying to get our attention. I looked up and saw the rhododendrons in our front yard bumping the glass. A gray sky blanketed what had been blue, so sudden a change, and now it might rain, even pour. When I stood to see the action, I noticed my father's car in the driveway. Really? During the Road Runner?

It was the first time in my life that I'd ever seen the man home before six on a weekday, and my immediate thought was a parent-teacher conference. Yikes. I could hear my teacher sighing before she spoke, "He daydreams, stares out at the trees, never seems engaged, and is constantly looking at the time, packing his things a half hour before the bell."

Please. No.

Did my father exist at 3:45 PM on a school day? was a question that hadn't been answered until now, so I stared at his Lincoln Continental, which I knew was making those panging noises under its wide, overheated hood. I asked my siblings if they knew why he was home and waited to hear his booming voice or the sound of his two thick briefcases as they pounded onto the floor in the front hall. Alex got up to see the car, and I sat on the couch next to my sister, ignoring the zoinks! and zowies! and the taps of the rhododendrons, because I needed to know where my father was. I knew it couldn't be good, the Lincoln in the driveway during cartoons, and then I thought it was a surprise, and then I thought he was away on a trip and had taken a cab, and then I heard the strangest thing: a yelp or a high scream, but not a woman's scream. A fierce and piercing shriek, a man's cry for life, and the eyes of my brother and sister leapt to me for answers, but my eyes searched theirs for the same.

Janice said something in a mumble, and the heavy thumping of feet raced down the back staircase like thundering guns, straight for the TV room, and silence would have found us but for the beep-beep of the Road Runner as my father's terrified face came into view. And he just glared at me, slack-jawed and pale, as I waited for the walls to crumble, the fire to spread.

"Take your brother and sister in the backyard," he said. "And don't come back until I tell you to."

It was bad. Whatever it was. And my skin tingled as the possibilities swirled in my brain. I knew this much: my tone with my brother and sister would need to reflect calm. I kept my voice high and friendly, as if we'd all just met. "Should we play a game? Who wants to go on the swings?"

As a leader, I was new, a rookie, wobbly-kneed but standing, and they both looked at me like a stranger.

"Good. Let's play on the swings," I repeated, and thought only of my father, picturing him entangled with a predator, a murderer, and where was Janice, poor Janice? Outside, I pointed at the jungle gym and asked Alex what he had done in school that day, and the absurdity of the question, coming from me, seemed to be the clincher for him. He began to cry, the tears building on themselves, his mouth wide now, the end of times. His sorrow thwarted our route to the swings, and I told them both that Dad would call us when it was time to come back and that there was nothing to worry about. Nothing at all. My sister looked back at the house and I guided them, my hands on their shoulders, farther into the yard.

"Look," I said, finding a dog-chewed Wiffle ball near the swings. Neither of them cared. The sky was silver and streaked with blackened clouds that were trading positions with bizarre speed. A storm. I tossed the ball to Rachel, and it landed at her feet. "Come on, throw it back."

"What's wrong?" she said. "Why was Dad scared?"

"I . . . didn't think that. There's nothing wrong. Throw it. Throw me the ball. Give me a pop up."

She didn't. She leaned to see the house.

"I want to go back," Alex said.

"What happened to Dad?" Rachel said and began to weep as well.

I walked to the ball and tossed it to Alex. It bumped his chest and fell to the grass. In my brother and sister's faces I saw my own thoughts. Doom. I told them to stop crying and to just toss me the stupid ball, but I knew something evil was unraveling back there, hovering over our things, our suburban safety. The gnawing of it all was in my throat and my knee-caps, and I, too, was beginning to freak. Was my dad hurt? Would we ever be the same? Frozen pizza, teacher conferences, and vacuums creating the buzzes of lazy weekday afternoons. Had the Road Runner ended? Was the TV engulfed in flames? Where was Janice standing, and would the zebra pillow be charred by the vicious bite of whatever scared my father into that hideous scream?

And then I remembered. Late the night before, my mother's mother had arrived from Australia and was staying in the guest room on the second floor. I'd only met her once when I was three, my siblings never, because she was an expat, a traveler, a woman we heard about at bedtime. She'd come home to the States because her second husband, Eric, had died suddenly while mowing his Australian lawn in his Australian town. In Australia. She was sick, she was dead, she was naked.

Had my father called my mother at work? The siren of

the ambulance was distant, like yet another suburban moan, and the years I had on my siblings alerted me first that it was headed toward us, our home. Their tears had subsided, and Alex was actually eyeing the swings as the siren got louder, more crisp. My sister stepped closer to the house, knowing that the ambulance was headed for us. She turned to me, and I could see her bottom teeth, which was odd since I didn't recognize them, so small, so hidden by her normal smile. She moved farther across the lawn, back to the house, and I loudly said, "Leap frog," to which Alex hit the dirt in gleeful anticipation of being hopped. I put my palms flat on his back and jumped over him, feigning a giggle, so much fun.

"Your turn! Jump over me now, buddy."

Rachel said, "Look," and there was no more hiding the loud red lights and screaming siren in our driveway, screeching to a stop behind the Lincoln. Paramedics hustled up our porch steps, and we all saw the front door swing wide.

The house was quiet as both my siblings squeaked, too scared to cry, and I heard familiar sounds over our neighbor's fence, a bark, a slammed screen door, as if no one had told the rest of the world that we were finished, ruined, slotted to suffer like families on the news.

The three of us stood in the driveway and stared at our tightly wrapped grandmother on the stretcher with orange straps. Defeated and pale, her white hair was matted and frayed, her eyelids closed. My father leaned down to her and said something in her ear before the men lifted her inside the ambulance. I don't think she heard what he said.

She'd scribbled love letters as the pills took effect, and

I saw them that evening as my mom and dad pieced them together, searching for information that would never come from her lips. Her dire words drooped off the lines of her powder-blue stationery and came to a scribbled ending at the bottom of the page. I rested my cheek against my mother's shoulder as she taped the torn edges of the note.

I didn't enter the room where it happened for months after my grandmother died. Like a roped-off crime scene, our guest room held a haunting beam that I could sometimes see beneath the crack in my bedroom door, just down the hall.

Ellio's pizza and the zoinks! and zowies! of a fast bird and a coyote strapped to a torpedo would forever remind me of my grandma's final minutes. I knew now about a sadness so vicious and unrelenting that a woman who loved us took her own life, as her daughter's children frolicked like puppies beneath her.

The cartoon was a facade, as were the vacuum, swing set, and shifting sky. A few weeks later I found myself sitting in front of the TV, blowing on my pizza as my siblings chased each other, falling into a tangle of little arms and sneakers. Janice was vacuuming, and the Road Runner had tied an anvil to a grand piano and strapped a rocket to it all, preparing to light the fuse.

"Beep-beep," he said, and Janice unplugged the vacuum.

I stood from the couch, and got on my toes to see if my dad's car was in the driveway. It wasn't. In fact there was no sound at all, except the very gentle tapping of the rhododendrons bumping against the glass.

MEASURING GRIEF

— Benita Garvin —

In 1980, I wrote my second stage play. My first was under submission to the Eugene O'Neill Festival, and I was not yet aware that it would become a finalist. My new play was about the death grip of a mother-daughter relationship. In my story, the daughter couldn't become her own person until she broke away from her controlling and competitive mother. The daughter resentfully works in the mother's chic clothing boutique, and their fragile relationship unravels when the daughter moves away and starts a new life. Years later, on the eve of winning an award for her first novel, she receives a call that her mother, unable to cope with her daughter's independence, has attempted suicide and has called her to her bedside.

In 2002, I was nominated for an Edgar Award for a film I wrote and produced. Days before, when I was to fly from Los Angeles, where I lived, to New York City to attend the black-tie event, I was awakened at the crack of dawn by a telephone call from a nurse in Florida with the news that my mother *and* my father had attempted suicide. In fact, they had made three attempts, all in the space of several hours, and failed, which is why they were in the hospital, rather than the morgue.

My mother was the de facto ringleader in the *folie à deux* that was my parents' marriage. When my eldest niece was ten years old, she asked the question that haunted me: what would happen to the remaining grandparent when the other one died? She felt certain one couldn't exist without the other. I was amazed that a child of ten could articulate my deepest fear and that someone so young, a child who saw my parents as infrequently as she did—perhaps twice a year—could sense the depth of their symbiosis.

My mother was a drama queen. Her death, or the threat of it, was perennially on the table. I remember her talking about putting her head in the oven or chiding me for digging her an early grave when I was a kid. As we both got older, the frequency of intimidations and threats of suicide increased, with my father joining her in the refrain.

My father was fun loving and easy going when I was growing up, but with age he became increasingly depressed and angry. The differences in my parents' personalities grew less distinguishable, until they seemed to merge into one. Like my mother, my father felt wronged and unappreciated. Together they struck back at the people and institutions they felt failed them by writing poison-pen letters, filing lawsuits, and picketing businesses.

The nurse on the phone informed me that the first of their three attempts occurred when they swallowed all the prescription medications in their house. At age eighty-seven and eighty-four respectively, my father and mother were in relatively good health. They had their share of ailments, and my father had come through a recent bout of colon cancer. Yet he hadn't had to endure chemotherapy or radiation and was given a 100 percent clean bill of health. Their maladies— high blood pressure, cholesterol, glaucoma, and so on—were common for people of their age. And although the required medications were expensive, they weren't lethal.

When the meds failed to achieve the desired effect, my parents moved into the closed garage, where they got into the car, turned on the ignition, and waited. Nothing happened. Finally, they returned to the house and, after a brief discussion, decided to slit their wrists. My mother couldn't bring herself to do it and pleaded with my father to do it for her. He refused. They found the sharpest kitchen knife, which most likely had been purchased at the ninety-nine-cent store years earlier and could barely cut paper, and attempted to slit their wrists. My mother cut vertically rather than horizontally, and neither of them cut deeply enough to sever a vein. All they succeeded in doing was making a bloody mess on the kitchen floor. They bled, waited, and bled some more, but they didn't die. That's when my father called 911.

As I spoke to the nurse, I inquired with apprehension about their conditions, expecting the nurse to say they were in comas or straitjackets. Instead, I was put through to my father, who sounded exactly as he might have sounded had I called in the middle of dinner. The timbre of his voice lent credibility to his claim that the entire incident was a "mistake." As we spoke, we were interrupted by my mother's voice on the extension.

With the three of us on the phone, they began to argue,

each disputing the facts surrounding their misguided suicide attempts. Here they were, literally in lockdown and under twenty-four-hour surveillance for having committed what the state of Florida deemed a crime, and they were fighting over whether it was his idea or hers. Had it been up to either of them, they would've simply checked out of what they seemed to think was an overpriced hotel with bad interior design and crappy food. And just try and get a night's sleep! Fortunately, they couldn't simply get up and walk: they were confined to the psychiatric wing.

It was surreal.

My mother's childhood, like my father's and others of their generation, was defined by the Great Depression. She grew up in brutal poverty wearing paper shoes to her school graduation. She was an only child in a loveless marriage. A photograph of her at age eight hanging on a wall in our home depicts a lonely little girl whose sad eyes had yet to dance with joy or laughter. Although it's sometimes hard to reconcile the bitter, angry person he was at the end of his life with the beloved funny man who would entertain the kids on our block with songs and stories when I was a child, my father's sense of humor was what first attracted her to him. Their fifty-plus-year marriage was an amalgam of love, loyalty, resentment, and utter devotion.

When people ask me why my parents attempted suicide, I usually say that it was depression. The truth is, it was a temper tantrum gone awry. Their bags were packed. They were on their way from Florida to Detroit, our hometown, with the intention of moving back for the third time. It was the middle of the night, and they were facing a ninety-minute drive to the Tampa airport and another hour waiting to pass through security.

This would've been the sixteenth or seventeenth move for my parents since retiring. They had spent two decades moving back and forth between Detroit, Florida, and Los Angeles. And once they settled in those cities, they proceeded to move within them. My mother was an interior designer, so it was assumed that she did it for business. To an outside observer, it might look like they were searching for the meaning of life, when in fact they were actually running from it.

On this particular night, facing the prospect of uprooting themselves yet again, my father was loading the suitcases into the car when my mother said she was too tired to face what was ahead. Rather than go back to bed, they opted for the Big Sleep. Out came the pills, and the madness began. It was that impetuosity, that spontaneous reckless behavior, and actions predicated on a whim that were at the root of the countless bad decisions my parents made over their lifetime, decisions that led them to run frantically around their house at four in the morning, a house they had just built and moved into, on their way to finding a new house in another part of the country.

A dangerous blend of fatigue, age, fear, a shrinking bank account, and profound neuroses caused them to suddenly change course and decide to end it all. What better way to punish the people they deemed responsible for their circumstances? They had just lost another lawsuit, one in which they invested what little remained in their savings; they were angry at the judge and the neighbors they had sued; they were angry at my brother for not agreeing to cosign on a new mortgage for them in Detroit; and they were angry at me because they were always angry at me.

They wanted to get our attention. And no amount of love from their children, grandchildren, or many friends satiated that need. My parents were determined to self-destruct.

My father used to tease my mother and say she was Japanese, because of her preoccupation with appearances and saving face. "What will [fill in the blank with a name] think?" was a mantra I heard as frequently as "Look before crossing the street." Growing up in the years before air-conditioning meant opening a window. My mother would scurry around the kitchen during dinner, a stifling heat outside, and close the windows to prevent our neighbors from hearing what might be construed as a small conflict or bad manners.

But there was no closing a window on this. Not only did their neighbors in Florida know, but their former neighbors in Michigan and Los Angeles found out through the snowbird hotline. There's nothing like a crisis or gossip to unite the flock. And, to my utter disbelief, neither parent felt the slightest bit of shame. To the contrary, my father had even taken a moment between the pills and the failed asphyxiation to compose a short note to my brother and me, saying we were great disappointments. It was as though they had been liberated from social conventions and now felt free to brazenly display their pain and vengeance.

Like the character in my play, I chose to attend the awards

ceremony rather than rush to my parents' bedside. I asked my brother, who lived with his family in San Francisco, to go in my place. (Whereas I was enmeshed with my parents and spent many years and thousands of dollars in therapy pursuing a relationship with my parents, he remained physically and emotionally estranged from them. During college, he distanced himself as far away in the United States as geography would permit.)

My brother didn't want to go but must have felt some sense of obligation and agreed to make the trip. I knew that his appearance would bolster their spirits, because it would be unexpected. They knew I'd show up; I was the girl, and gender determined the balance of relationships in our family. Being a girl, I was a known entity to my mother. She could take me shopping, show me how to dress, how to wear my hair and makeup, and the rest of the time anguish about the kind of man I would marry. But my brother was a mystery to her.

She once recounted the first time she saw him—or rather this foreign object called a penis—and she was terrified. What to say or do with a creature who bore this appendage? The only memory I have of my mother relating to my brother is when she'd drag him to the boys' store in our neighborhood and outfit him with new clothes.

By the time my brother arrived in Florida, my parents had been separated and were on different floors. Although it wasn't initially apparent, that very act was enough to sever the cord. My father seemed to be doing well, but then he fell out of bed in the middle of the night in an attempt to go to the bathroom. A subsequent physical examination, x-rays, and other tests didn't turn up any injuries, yet he inexplicably lost his ability to speak coherently.

I arrived several days after the awards ceremony to relieve my brother from duty. I shuffled between my parents' rooms, sleeping in a chair in my father's room so I could be there in case he spoke. The doctor felt it was only a matter of time until his voice returned or they figured out what was wrong. There was nothing more to do until they were finally released from the hospital. I flew back to Los Angeles, confident that my parents, although not yet out of the woods, would survive.

Several nights later, I got a call from my brother. "He's gone."

I learned from a nurse that my mother had seen my father only hours before his death. The visit was their first since their separation, and it would prove to be their last. He had been unconscious, but when she leaned over and kissed him, he responded. Later that night, my mother awoke with a start from her drug-induced sleep and let out a cry. It was just after midnight, the exact time my father, two floors above, died. My mother's worst fantasy, and mine, had happened.

The news of my father's death threw my mother's future, as well as my own, into question. My parents had sold their house and had to be out of it in a week. Where would my mother live? She was homeless, with little money, and she was suicidal. And, given her fragile state of mind, she was in no position to make any decisions. Her life was now in my hands.

If you're going to commit suicide, it's best to stick to the method that is most likely to produce the desired result. A bullet to the head or through the mouth, for example, is probably the best choice. Pills are definitely the worst option. Not that I knew that before this incident. To the contrary, I assumed that if you ingested a bottle of sleeping pills, you were a goner. Not so. Chances are quite good you'll end up a vegetable rather than a corpse. In the weeks after my father's death, I became an expert on the subject of suicide.

I returned to Florida. We honored my father's wishes and had him cremated. I spent several days alone in their house, going through their belongings. That's when I found the note telling my brother and me that we had failed as his children. Somewhere between the pills and the garage, he had mustered enough anger to toss out one final zinger. As I sat there knee-deep in the physical, financial, and emotional mess that he and my mother had created, I was struck by the cruelty and the irony of his sentiment.

I brought my mother back to California with instructions from her physician that I was to take her directly to a facility for psychiatric evaluation. She had committed a crime and was also considered a high suicide risk. The Florida hospital had made arrangements to transfer her to the Cedars-Sinai psychiatric unit in Los Angeles. The good news was that with her in safe hands, I could start to find her an apartment and, hopefully, some backup resources to assist her in creating a new life.

My loving and supportive husband picked us up at the Los Angeles airport. I hoped that my mother would not realize it was her wedding anniversary. However, she discovered it when she signed the hospital forms and had to ask the date. Until then, she had been docile. With knowledge of the special date, however, she snapped out of her lethargy and begged us not to leave her there. My husband, who always had a calming influence on her, explained that remaining was a condition of her release, that we'd return in the morning, and that her stay was temporary. Nothing we said calmed her. She promised to be good, sleep on the floor, or do anything we asked, as long as we didn't leave her there. In my eyes, she had become a child who blames herself when her parents abandon the family.

Later that day, when my husband and I returned home from the hospital, we held each other and sobbed until we ran out of tears.

My brother and I knew that once my mother was released from the hospital she would try again to kill herself, and she would keep trying until she succeeded. The question was what to do about it. He saw two choices: we could institutionalize her, where she could be monitored, or we could police her ourselves around the clock. My brother opted for the former. He didn't want her to be his responsibility, and didn't understand why I'd want her to be mine. "You'll walk in some morning and find her dead," he told me. "You know that, don't you?" Maybe he felt that our mother should live with the consequences of her behavior as some kind of retribution. "She brought this all on herself."

I couldn't argue with that. She'd been the instigator, but it was my father who died. I knew she couldn't live with the guilt. That's why she couldn't bear going on another day, and locking her in some psychiatric ward seemed unbearably cruel and a far more painful death.

Understanding this, I believed her fate was a foregone conclusion: she was going to find a way to end her life. Nevertheless, I had to let her determine this for herself. My mother was an adult. It was her life. If she didn't want to live, what right did I or the state of California have to force her to live? Despite everything, I loved my mother, and I wanted to keep her alive. I told myself that I'd give her as much love and support as possible and hope she might choose to live out her *natural* life. Anything was possible. It's the same magical thinking and eternal optimism that has kept me in the movie business all these years.

Another thing I learned about suicide is that, unlike illness, it's not neutral; suicide is accompanied by stigma and judgment. Tell someone that so-and-so died of cancer, and they'll be sympathetic. Tell them that death came from jumping off a ledge, and you'll get wide-eyed stares and macabre curiosity.

I was riddled with pain and guilt and was desperate to talk about it, yet I didn't want to talk to my husband or friends. It had nothing to do with how close I felt to them; it was that I needed people who were going through *exactly* what I was going through. My brother and I were having the same experience, but our family dynamic didn't foster intimacy and closeness between siblings.

The only other family was my father's two sisters, but they had a long, contentious, on-again, off-again relationship with my parents. And, despite having been in "on" mode prior to their brother's suicide, they went MIA and never sent so much as a condolence card to my mother.

I remembered that a young friend's girlfriend had asphyxiated herself after he broke up with her. He attended a suicide support group and found it invaluable to his healing. I decided to do the same. I'd spent a good deal of my adult life in and out of therapy, and I'm comfortable in a therapeutic environment.

The suicide grief support group was time-limited, ten weeks, and part of a long-established mental health organization that was highly regarded in the Los Angeles area. Although my group was not racially diverse, it was diverse in other respects, such as age, income, and geography, with an equal ratio of men and women. What bound us was the specific shame and guilt that are the hallmarks of suicide survivors. At our first meeting, we went around the room to introduce ourselves and reveal the nature of the loved one's suicide.

I admit that I possessed a large dose of the macabre curiosity I ridiculed in others. In these sessions, I listened intently to each member recount their tale. I listened as an outsider, insider, a writer, voyeur, shrink, and survivor. A heavyset guy in his mid-thirties, with dancing eyes and a warm smile, told us how he got a call that his father, whom he hadn't seen or spoken to in months, had slit his wrists and was found in a tub full of blood. He blamed himself for not being a better son.

A petite, impeccably dressed, soft-spoken woman in her forties, who lived a cultured, enviable life of financial comfort, told of coming home from work and finding her husband hanging in their bedroom. Hoping he might still be alive, she cut down his six-foot body, only to have it fall on top of her, pinning her to the ground. Despite the fact that, the day before, they had enjoyed a night out on the town to celebrate their anniversary, she blamed herself for not being a better wife.

A sixty-year-old mother and widow had been coming to these groups for seven years. Her only son had overdosed from heroin. They had always been extremely close, and unlike my father, who had left behind a sentence or two blaming my brother and me for their actions, her son had left her a beautiful, loving letter "gifting" her the only thing that meant anything to him: his dog. She blamed herself for not seeing the signs.

A young mother in her late twenties lived with her husband and newborn baby in a high-rise apartment in downtown Los Angeles. Her sister was going through a nasty divorce and had moved in, planning to stay until she got herself sorted out. It was great for the new mom because her sister adored the baby and was very helpful with the chores. One night, this sister went out on an errand and didn't come back. She had taken the elevator to the top of the building and jumped. The distraught young mother said she was in this group to figure out what she had done to make her sister do this.

As I ranked the stories, the worst was the pregnant twenty-six-year-old whose husband asphyxiated himself. It made me wonder if there was a pattern emerging: asphyxiation seemed to be the method du jour for the thirty-and-under set. So why didn't it work for my parents? Were they too old?

It was all too complicated.

As I sat there ranking these personal tragedies based on their level of drama and loss—always the screenwriter—I began to wonder what kind of person I was. From as far back as I can remember, my mother compared me to my friends or her friends' children. It began with my beloved friend and neighbor, Barbara King. My mother never understood why I didn't keep myself as neat as Barbara. It started there, but it never ended.

As I grew up, I picked up where my mother left off, always holding myself up to others and coming up short. Now I had real evidence of my worthlessness: I measured people's grief. I weighed their suffering or guilt against mine, and it made me feel better. It also filled me with shame, so I kept the "game" I was playing to myself.

Once released from the hospital and living in her own apartment, my mother made another failed suicide attempt. I took her to more doctors, and they adjusted her antidepressant meds—as if she didn't have ample reason to be depressed. I even convinced her to attend a senior grief counseling group. True to the maxim "Let no good deed go unpunished," my mother returned from that grief group further regressed, because a widower ten years her junior had hit on her. She was an extremely vain and beautiful woman who, with her square jaw, high cheeks, and creamy skin looked gorgeous at every age. A man, let alone a younger man, finding her attractive would normally delight her, but she viewed this romantic advance with horror. She would never be comfortable with another man. She didn't want another man. She wanted my father. She never returned to the group.

What scared me most was that she would do it again, incorrectly, and leave herself in a vegetative or equally horrific condition. She didn't announce the date or the time; she didn't have to. It wasn't a matter of *if* my mother would kill herself, only when.

Meanwhile, I was meant to fly to Washington, DC, to accept a media award from the American Bar Association. Once again life imitated my stage play. I was about to receive recognition for my achievement as a writer and a producer of a film, and instead of enjoying the moment, I was upstaged by another parental crisis. I secured a vow from my mother that she wouldn't try and off herself in my absence. I then arranged for her to stay at the home of a widow she'd known for many years.

When I got to Washington, I couldn't relax. I was eager to pick up the award and go home. Anytime I heard a phone ring, I jumped. During the ceremony, my thoughts drifted to my father. He'd gone to law school, but after the war he went into business. It's what the clever young Jewish men were doing when they came home. If ever there was a man not cut out for business, it was he, as his subsequent fortunes bore out. His "failure" (as he always referred to it) had reversed itself in recent years. He came out of retirement and began to practice law, preparing wills, handling easy divorces, and such. He was enormously proud of this accomplishment and particularly pleased because it brought in much-needed income. I wondered if he'd be proud that his daughter was receiving an award from the group he held in such high esteem.

Sitting in that room in DC, it finally struck me: the battle was over, and I had lost. I would never have my parents' approval. Nothing I had done before or would do in the future would change that. Even faced with what he believed were his final moments on earth, all my father could leave my brother and me were a few cruel words. There would be no tearful goodbyes, no expressions of love, regrets, or missed opportunities—the chapter with my father was closed.

My mother's final chapter was still a work in progress.

I returned to Los Angeles and found my mother exactly as I left her—eager and ready to join my father. Again, I urged my brother to fly down and see her one last time, but he declined.

The following day, my brother's premonition came true. I found my mother's body. She was clever and had bought a book on suicide, which signaled to the world, primarily me, that she was serious. I cut the plastic bag from her face, in the event she was still alive. She wasn't. She appeared to be asleep. Her cheek felt cool and smooth, like marble. I kissed her forehead and apologized. I told her that I was sorry that she had been so unhappy, that her life hadn't turned out the way she'd dreamed, that she'd never believed or understood how much I loved her and would miss her. I left the apartment as I found it, in case the police wanted to check the glass where she had mixed sleeping pills and alcohol. And then I went home, an orphan.

To understand what comes next, you must understand my grief yardstick. I'm crappy at math, so I couldn't quantify it, but I put my situation as worse than Heroin-Overdosed Son, but not nearly as bad as Young Pregnant Widow. In any case, it was time to return to my suicide group, and I was going to walk in and trump everyone. Even Young Pregnant Widow. I was not happy about this. I considered avoiding the subject, or casually referencing it in the course of a story, something like "...with both parents gone..." But it seemed counterproductive to be in a suicide group and not mention the fact that your mother had just joined your father in heaven or hell or, in the case of my parents, in an urn on my piano. I considered saving my mother's suicide for the next group that was being formed, but I didn't want to spend another ten weeks measuring a fresh batch of guilty grievers. I had no choice.

It was customary for the leader, herself a survivor, to ask if anybody had anything they would like to say. We had recently passed a milestone: when the leader asked that question the last several weeks, somebody had always spoken up. Not so this time. Everybody shifted in their seats, looked at their hands or feet. It was as though the silence screamed out to me to speak, telling me the longer I waited to make the announcement, the more difficult it would be.

"I'd like to say something." I then proceeded to do what my husband always accuses me of, qualifying what comes next. "I realize this isn't a competition. I mean, I'm not trying to upstage anybody." I took a deep breath and continued, "My mother killed herself the night before last."

It was a hot summer night in a building that had no airconditioning. The fluorescent overhead lighting buzzed, emitting heat and radiation, making the already stifling environment even more so. Forget the bullshit that dry heat is better. Extreme heat *sans* humidity is just as miserable. It was claustrophobic. The room was so quiet I could hear people sweating. Finally, after what felt like an eternity, the man whose father had died in the tub said, "Well, that's a show-stopper."

The room erupted into laughter. Even the group leader couldn't restrain herself from joining in. It was as if somebody had pricked a balloon, releasing all the air. Tears rolled down the faces of people whom I had never seen manage the slightest of smiles. It marked a turning point for the group. Because despite all the intimacy that such a group implies, we had not yet allowed ourselves to laugh in our time of unimaginable grief, for fear we'd be seen as callous or cruel. Breaking that unspoken taboo liberated us. Before this moment, we were connected by grief. Now, we were connected by something equally as powerful: laughter.

Once we crossed that boundary, the remaining walls tumbled down, and we became a cohesive group. On the last meeting, we sat together and candidly looked back on our journeys. Each of us confessed measuring our grief against the others!

It was suggested that we take a vote to determine which of us had the most tragic tale. We embraced the idea. Ballots were cast, and the votes tallied. We shared our last group belly laugh when the winner was announced: Young Pregnant Widow was a clean sweep.

I left the group struck by the banality of death, even when it's a more lurid death like suicide. The truth is, however we leave this world, we've left it. Death, in all its forms, was finally demystified for me. And I learned that even in grief there can be moments of humor. I also found out that my reactions— from what made me cry to what me laugh—were not unique, they were universal. It was a humbling experience.

My fears, guilt, and grief were very much like those emotions experienced by everyone in my group. And even my shameful secret, which was my proclivity to secretly quantify death, was also shared. I went in thinking I was different, and I came out seeing that I'm very much like everyone else, ordinary in the most extraordinary way. And it was the ordinariness that made it extraordinary. I was human.

DECCA'S POTTY

— Kathi Kamen Goldmark —

I could tell you how we met.

I arrived to escort an author to a television interview and ended up sitting in a Berkeley kitchen with Maya Angelou and Jessica Mitford telling me about riding elephants together in a charity circus parade—two of the world's best storytellers comparing their fantasies of wearing spangled harem pants and lounging in pillowed luxury versus the reality of being hoisted up to terrifying heights and hanging on for dear life. The elephants' hide was rough. "It turns out you have to wear the stoutest of jeans," giggled Mitford, the world-renowned muckraking journalist, former card-carrying member of the Communist Party, legendary civil-rights activist, and author of *The American Way of Death,* a book that revolutionized the funeral industry.

I could tell you about the first performance.

I had been asked to help recruit authors for a literary talent show to celebrate the fortieth anniversary of the *Paris Review,* and it happened that Maya Angelou was in town. I invited her to stay for a few extra days so she could be in the show.

"Hmmm," she said. "I can't stay that long, but Decca will do it. Have you ever heard her sing 'Maxwell's Silver Hammer'?

No? Well then . . ." Dr. Angelou picked up the car phone and dialed a number. "Decca," she said. "I've bought you a scholarship. You're going to be in a show. Here, talk to Ms. Goldmark."

That was how I met Jessica Mitford (known to her friends and family as "Decca") and became her record producer.

She arrived at the *Paris Review* party in a glittery gown. My band was performing, and we did a journeyman's job of backing up Leticia Baldridge on "La Vie en Rose," Ben Fong-Torres on a couple of Elvis tunes, and Louis B. Jones and Nion McEvoy on a classic rocker. Herb Caen contributed jazzy drum stylings. We let George Plimpton plow through "The Minute Waltz" on his own. But Decca brought down the house singing "Maxwell's Silver Hammer" with Caen on cowbell. I looked over at David, my musical coconspirator and bandleader. He nodded. We had to record this for posterity. That's how "Don't Quit Your Day Job" Records was born— and went on to achieve CD sales well into the dozens—with Decca and the Dectones as our first project.

I could tell you about the recording session.

I couldn't afford the gorgeous horn section required to duplicate the music bed on the Beatles' arrangement of "Maxwell's Silver Hammer," so I invited twenty Jessica Mitford fans to join us on kazoo instead. The Dectones, as we called them, performed double-duty on a second track, "The Ballad of Grace Darling," a song Decca had learned in her youth that featured a large group howling "Help! Help!" on the chorus. We released Decca's single with a blowout bash at San Francisco's Paradise Lounge featuring a half-hour set of old protest songs, torch songs, and the grand finale, "The Ballad of Decca," a parody which, in true old-Commie form, was written by committee with her husband, labor lawyer Bob Treuhaft. Sung to the tune of "Grace Darling," it was the story of Decca's life, minus the elephant ride:

THE BALLAD OF DECCA

(To be sung to the tune of "Grace Darling."
Lyrics by Kathi Goldmark, Bob Treuhaft,
Audrey deChadenedes, and Tony Goldmark.)

*'Twas on the grounds of Swinbrook, there dwelt an
    English maid*
Pure as the air around her, of danger ne'er afraid
A prisoner of the nursery, as bored as she could be
So, longing for adventure, she split with Romilly—and—
She sailed away o'er the rolling sea, over the waters blue
"HELP! HELP!" she could hear the cries of a cause so true
Decca was very smart, integrity she craved
She pulled away o'er the rolling spray, and her life she saved
She settled in Oakland's flatlands, accepting many a dare
With Dinky, Bob, and Benjy, determined to make things fair
When the Unamericans rode into town,
Decca was there with a wink and a frown
*Taking the fifth (which became a noun) she never let her
    comrades down—and—*
*Fearlessly she sailed into the fray—relentlessly brave
    and true*
"HELP! HELP!" she could hear the cry
That echoed around and pierced the sky

But she was ready with her reply, "You'll never get me
    to testify"
But when she sang the Beatles, her life turned upside-down
With "Maxwell" and "Grace Darling" she makes
    a lovely sound
So madly looking forward to singing here tonight
Let's put our hands together for England's brightest light—
    as—
She sails away o'er chorus and verse, accompanied by kazoo
"HELP! HELP!" you can hear the cries of the Dectones,
    too
With a true performer's heart, and vocals strong and brave
She'll sing today in her dashing way
And the show she'll save!

The kazoo chorus, proud Dectones all, became a signature component of the "Don't Quit Your Day Job" sound, and I learned how to record and mix kazoo sound with an ambience of controlled chaos—a lost art, these days.

I could tell you about taking the show on the road.
    Decca, Maya Angelou, and journalist Shana Alexander headlining a lit-rock event in Cary, North Carolina, along with Olivia Goldsmith and Roy Blount, Jr.; a gala at Slim's to close the San Francisco Book Festival; a performance at the opening of the new San Francisco Public Library; a very strange gig on the roof of Virgin Records downtown, with Cyndi Lauper as the headliner; a glorious evening on the stage of Town Hall in New York on behalf of the *Nation* magazine; a CD release

party in an Upper East Side New York town house; a follow-up recording, *There Is a Moral to It All: Musical Duets*, with Maya Angelou and Jessica Mitford singing English music hall ditties "Right, Said Fred" and "One Fish Ball." There were always eager kazoo-tooting Dectones backing up our star, well into her seventies, giving "Maxwell's Silver Hammer" her all before an enchanted crowd.

And I could tell you about singing old union songs with Decca and Bob in their Berkeley living room.

Hearing great stories about standing up to the House Un-American Activities Committee and the early days of the American Communist Party; many delightful parties and dinners. I read her autobiographies and learned about the famously well-documented Mitford sisters and her extraordinary life.

Decca was the daughter of the Second Baron Redesdale, born in Burford, Oxfordshire, in 1917. She was a self-described autodidact, educated at home by her mother. She told me about her sisters: Diana Mitford, who married Oswald Mosley, leader of the British Union of Fascists; Unity Mitford, who became a close friend of Adolf Hitler; Nancy Mitford, "the *real* writer in the family." Decca developed left-wing sensibilities. She married Esmond Romilly, nephew of Winston Churchill, and the couple moved to the United States in 1939. Romilly joined the Royal Canadian Air Force and was killed in a bombing raid.

A few years later, Mitford married radical lawyer Robert Treuhaft. They both joined the American Communist Party and were active in the Civil Rights movement. They moved to Oakland in 1948 and had lived in the East Bay ever since, raising kids, fighting for social justice and the rights of the oppressed, and writing scathing, hilarious exposés.

We became great pals.

Meanwhile, I'd caught the record-producer bug and began working on other projects. Of all the quirky offerings on the "Don't Quit Your Day Job" label, Decca's favorite was the album *Potty Animal: Funny Songs about Potty Training.* She offered a blurb for the back panel and sent me cassettes of scatological ditties she'd collected from all over the world.

Fast-forward to KPFA's Berkeley studio, sometime in 1996. David Gans invited Decca and me to appear as guests on his Grateful Dead–themed radio show. We agreed, lured by the promise that we could bring our own music to play on the air. As Decca cued up her choice, *Potty Animal,* we could feel Deadheads turning off their radios in droves.

A few months later, Decca went to the doctor with peculiar symptoms and was diagnosed with brain cancer. She had just a few weeks to gather her loved ones around her, to settle her affairs, and to deliver marching orders to those of us who visited her bedside—amounting to instructions on how to take care of one another after she was gone.

I led my band of loyal Dectones, kazoos in hand, in a final tribute at the memorial, a spectacular event. Then I went home to try to figure out how to fill the empty space. No more playful faxes filled with corny jokes, or thanks for the "swell grub" after a dinner party. No more thrilling moments on lead kazoo, holding up the "Bang! Bang!" and "Help! Help!"

sing-along signs beside my lovely star as she bellowed and vamped her heart out. No more Decca. And without Decca, there could be no more Dectones.

A couple of weeks later, I got a call from Bob.

"Can you come by this week? There's something that Decca wanted you to have."

We made a date, and I wondered what the something might be. A trinket? A book? A letter about all the fun we'd had pretending to be rock stars together? Bob wouldn't give any clues, and a few days later I drove to Berkeley to pick up what I was sure would be a small gift, a token.

He pointed to an old, polished hardwood cabinet in the hallway. "That's it," he said with a smile. "I hope you have room in your trunk."

"Um, wow, thanks."

"Do you know what this is? Here, let me show you." The front of the cabinet turned out to be two fake drawers on a hinged covering. Bob removed the facade to reveal—a porcelain potty.

"It's the Mitford family chamber pot. Decca loved your potty songs, and she wanted you to have this. It's over a hundred years old, you know."

I wrestled my treasure into the car, thinking of all the aristocratic English bottoms that had graced this gift, going back over a hundred years. It remains in a place of honor in my dining room to this day, adorned with a 45 of Bernard Cribbins singing "Right, Said Fred" and a photo of Decca at her

CD release party. Using a pair of red flannel cowboy boxer shorts as a hanky, she wipes her eyes while vamping on "Mean to Me," her favorite torch song.

The commode itself, of course, is filled with kazoos.

MY PET DEAD MOLE

— Zoe FitzGerald Carter —

It's early spring in Northern California—roadkill season—and it's the fifth dead skunk I've passed on my bike this morning. This one is perfect, though, with no obvious signs of violence or bloodshed. Casually curled up at the edge of the road, it looks like it's just fallen asleep. I have a sudden urge to stop, get off my bike, check it out, see what its face and its little skunk paws look like up close. Maybe even see how long its body is, if I stretch it out.

I don't stop. I am aware that it is neither hygienic nor completely normal to want to examine dead animals. But as I continue down the road, I realize that such conventional concerns haven't always stopped me. In fact, there was a time—an incident really—when I gave full rein to my interest in dead animals.

It was the year I turned nine, and I had flown with my family from Washington, DC, to Castle Park, Michigan, to spend spring break with my grandfather. He lived in an enormous yellow house that was part of a secluded enclave of palatial "cottages" along the shores of Lake Michigan. It was a lovely, old-fashioned house with multiple staircases, a vast sleeping porch, and a basement that reeked of the oversized rubber inner tubes that we hauled down to the lake each day. Adding to this exotic splendor was the endless, perfectly maintained lawn, complete with wending stone walls and a white wrought-iron bench around one of the trees.

My grandfather was very particular about his lawn. In fact, unbeknownst to me, he had recently set out several spring-loaded traps to deal with an influx of burrowing moles. Out playing in the garden one afternoon, my sister, Sarah, and I were startled when my grandfather abruptly stepped out of the house, walked quickly across the lawn, and pulled up a trap from a hole in the ground. In its steel maw was a dead, but perfectly intact, baby mole. I asked my grandfather to let me see him and promptly fell in love. He was soft and tiny and utterly perfect, with sleek dark brown fur and a sweet closed-eyed little face.

At this point, my memory grows a bit hazy. How to explain the fact that the dead mole wasn't whisked away and tossed into the woods, or deposited in some unceremoniously dug shallow grave? All I know is that somehow, once I got my hands on him, he was mine. My only explanation is that it was the late sixties and my parents were "progressive" in their approach to child rearing, believing it was more important that my two sisters and I be interesting rather than conventional.

Eventually, they did insist I put the mole in a plastic bag and stick him in my grandfather's freezer, but only after promising that I could bring him back to DC when we flew home later that week. In the meantime, I found every excuse to nip into the kitchen and check on him. This usually involved taking him out of the box and balancing him on the table in a standing position, holding his frozen paws between my fingertips. If the coast was clear and I had time to linger, I would walk him past the sugar bowl and saltshaker, and even have him execute a few turns and pirouettes.

Getting into the kitchen was nerve-wracking, however, because I lived in fear of running into my gruff, stooped, old grandfather. Despite his frail frame, my grandpa had a grumpy, intimidating demeanor. He always seemed to have a cigar in his mouth and, whenever he drove us somewhere in his big shiny Chrysler, he would gesture impatiently at the driver in front of him and mutter, "Tromp on the old mushroom!" And while I loved my mole—despite its being dead—I couldn't help thinking my grandfather a bit mean for having killed him.

By the time we were ready to fly home, my parents had taken an "Isn't this hilarious?" attitude toward the whole thing, and my father thought it especially amusing that we had tucked the mole into a box that had "Figgy Pudding" printed on it. Once on the airplane, he asked the stewardess to put it in the refrigerator, which—this *was* the 1960s—she did. He then looked very pleased with himself and made jokes about what might happen if she got hungry and decided to steal some pudding.

Meanwhile, I thought about my dead mole the whole way home, still astonished that I'd been allowed to keep him. As soon as we were in the taxi from the airport, I opened his box and was delighted to find that he had thawed enough for me to take him out and sit him on my lap. I loved that I could be so close to him (for some reason it never crossed my mind that "he" might have been female) and couldn't stop looking at his little hands and feet, his tiny black nose.

"You really *are* weird, Zoe," Sarah said, in her big sister voice. She was only a year older but had given up playing with stuffed animals, so of course she wouldn't understand. "And that dead animal," she said, poking at my mole's flattened ears, "is disgusting."

"He is not," I answered indignantly. "It's not *his* fault he's dead."

Actually, while I never would've admitted it, being dead was part of what made him so intriguing. The fact that he was a real animal, with fur and bones and blood, meant he was more "real" than my stuffed animals with their plastic eyes and foam insides. But being dead also made him less real than, say, our family dog. And so he existed in this strange middle place—more exciting than a toy, but not as thrilling as a live animal—and yet somehow *more* thrilling, because having him allowed me to quite literally get my hands around death, a topic that had long obsessed me.

For months, I'd been driving my family crazy asking them if they would rather be shot or hanged, burned or drowned, left on a desert island with no food or attacked by a wild animal. I never understood why they would invariably tell me to go away, apparently not as fascinated by these hypothetical scenarios as I was. I think in my own way I was trying to understand death and, at the same time, manage my anxiety about it. Gruesome as my questions were, they assumed that we would have a choice about how we died and that we might even be

able to pick the least painful or distressing option. My dead
mole functioned similarly. Intact and seemingly unchanged by
death—other than the fact that he couldn't move on his own,
of course—my mole somehow made death *okay*.

By the time we got home, I had named him Moley, in honor
of Ratty in *The Wind in the Willows*. Moley went right into the
freezer when we arrived, but when Monday morning came, I
impulsively decided to take him to school. My friends were
always bringing their pets to school for show-and-tell, so I
had the brilliant idea of telling my parents that I was taking
Moley in for this reason, even though there was no such event
that day. I did want to show him off, but I also didn't want to
leave him alone in the freezer all day.

My teacher, Miss Hopper, was a high-strung woman with
poppy eyes and a buzzing, nervous energy that always made
me feel exhausted. But I liked her and felt that, as one of the
few young, unmarried teachers in the school, she wouldn't
mind so much if I brought a dead animal to class. But when
I opened up the Figgy Pudding box, she immediately asked if
my parents knew what I had brought to school.

"Oh, yes," I told her confidently. "They told me I could
bring him." I scooped Moley up and—stroking his fur with
one hand—held him out to show her. "See how cute he is,
Miss Hopper? You can pat him if you want."

"Oh, sweetie, that's okay," she said, her poppy eyes even
wider than usual as she stared down at him. "It's really not
hygienic to handle dead animals. In fact, why don't you go
wash your hands? Right now, honey. Just put him right back

into that box and give him to me. You can show him to the class before lunchtime."

When I returned to my desk a few minutes later, a boy I didn't like very much said, "Ew, you brought a dead rat to school?"

"Noooo," I said, angrily. "It's a *mole!*"

"That's gross," he sneered.

Turning my back on him, I tried to focus on my addition worksheet, but I felt a little worried. *Was* Moley gross? I thought about the gingerly way Miss Hopper had carried him across the room and the fact that he was sitting on the very top shelf behind her desk. I also remembered my sister sneering at him in the cab. But then I remembered the way Moley's fur grew in a perfect little swirl under his arms and the way it looked like he had a potbelly when I made him sit on my lap. I didn't care what other people thought: Moley was mine and I loved him.

My instinct to stand by my mole paid off when I got to tell the whole class about how my grandfather had killed him and how I had managed to get a hold of him and bring him home on the plane. Miss Hopper looked very solemn and said it was "really, really sad" when something died—even a wild animal. Everyone was quiet and serious-looking as I walked around with him, and a couple of kids looked like they might cry. Even when one of them darted their hand into his box to pat him and was abruptly sent off to the restroom to wash, the atmosphere remained subdued. This only made me feel more important. Other kids talked about going to beaches in Florida or watching TV on their vacation, but no one had a story as interesting as mine.

My exhilaration was only slightly dimmed when, just before I left the room for lunch, Miss Hopper pulled me aside and quietly asked that I *not* bring Moley back to school. "You might want to give him a nice burial in your backyard this afternoon, sweetie," she said firmly. "I think he's been through enough."

Put Moley in the ground? I thought. No way! Obviously, Miss Hopper was just being "conventional." I wasn't actually sure what the word meant, but I was pretty sure it explained why she thought I should get rid of Moley.

At lunch, several of the boys wanted to talk to me about "that dead animal you got," and I found myself showing off a little, referring to Moley the same way and talking about how my parents didn't mind that I had him. Then, in my group violin class that afternoon, our teacher, Miss Aubrey, who was old and ill-tempered, was late to class, and I slipped Moley out of his box to show everyone. For a few glorious moments, I was surrounded by kids, all of whom had promptly dropped their violins and raced over. As they passed him around, several of the girls cooed, "He's soooo cute," and I once again felt proud to have him in my possession. The whole idea that his being dead was disgusting or upsetting was totally forgotten.

When the door opened and Miss Aubrey walked in, I had to think fast. I knew she was going to have a fit if she saw Moley, so I ducked down, grabbed my violin out of its case, and dropped Moley inside. All the kids laughed as I sat back up and began flipping through my Suzuki book, pretending to tune my violin.

"Children, please! Be quiet!" Miss Aubrey said, looking suspiciously at me over her glasses. "Zoe, is there something you want to share with the rest of us?"

Again, the room erupted into excited whispers and giggles, and I began to sweat, sure that someone was going to let it slip that I had a dead mole in my violin case. And I had another source of worry: Moley had definitely begun to smell. Not bad exactly, but a distinct odor. I hoped it didn't start to spread around the room, which was already stuffy and over-heated. "Oh no, Miss Aubrey. Everything's fine." I assumed a bland, disinterested expression and, once she turned away, shot a fierce warning look at the two grinning boys sprawled in the seats behind me. As the class proceeded, I sat in a paroxysm of anxiety that either the smell—or one of my classmates—would give me away.

Back at home that afternoon, my mother insisted Moley go immediately back into the freezer, and by the time I got home the next afternoon I was feeling tired and grouchy and only peeked in on him briefly. While I would never have admitted it, Moley wasn't looking so cute anymore. Somehow his day at school had leached the gloss from his coat, and he had frozen into a strange shape, with one paw bent at a spastic-looking angle. Another day passed without my taking him out to play, and another after that. By then, my interest in him had definitely begun to wane, although I thought about him often, missing those first exhilarating days after he came into my possession.

Then, a few weeks later, my mother came into my room look-ing excited. She had been telling her friend, Sally, about "our mole saga," as she called it, and Sally had suggested we get in touch with Laney Dexter, a teenager who lived a couple of blocks over. Laney was an eccentric girl with glasses and messy hair who always reminded me of Meg Murry in *A Wrinkle in Time.* Just like brainy, odd Meg, Laney had some unusual interests, including, apparently, taxidermy. She had been teach-ing herself how to dry and stuff animals so as to preserve them and had apparently been practicing on various recently deceased pets from around the neighborhood.

"So I was thinking we could see if Laney could stuff your mole," my mother said brightly. "That way, you can keep it, but you don't have to worry about having him ... *decompose.*"

My mother looked so delighted with the idea that I agreed, although I didn't feel very enthusiastic. I'd been to taxidermy shops up in New England during summer vacations, and the animals there always looked dusty and sad. What I wanted was Moley to be soft and fresh again so I could play with him. I thought about the word *decompose* and suddenly felt like crying. I knew what decompose meant. It was when things turned mushy and moldy, like old fruit when it's been on the counter too long. I hadn't minded so much that Moley was dead, as long as he looked alive. But now I realized that, instead of staying the way he'd been at the moment of death, Moley was going to rot and turn into something awful. It was a prospect I didn't want to contemplate.

That weekend, we took him over to the Dexters' house, and Laney agreed to work on him. I should have known I was never going to see Moley again when I caught a glimpse of eight or nine frozen little packages all lined up next to each other in her freezer, but by then it was too late to snatch him back.

And sure enough, I never did get Moley back. Laney must have accrued quite a backlog of dead animals because, over the years, I've run into other people from the neighborhood who told me that they, too, handed over their deceased pets, never to see them again. But then, I suppose having my mole stuffed by a self-taught teenage taxidermist might have been worse than having him trapped in her freezer forever. And frankly, I was ready to let him go by then.

What I wasn't ready to let go of was my interest in death. I continued to back my family into corners to grill them on their preferred way to die, and I found death scenes in movies and books of enormous interest. Like many children, I was curious about death and not sure yet if I should be afraid of it. Even when my grandfather died the following year, I remained more interested than sad. Mainly, I thought a lot about his body and was deeply relieved to hear he'd been embalmed, which apparently meant he wouldn't decompose. At least for a while.

Years later, when my father died from cancer at the age of sixty-eight, and my mother ended her life after a long struggle with Parkinson's disease, I would get a crash course in death's concomitant companions, grief and loss. And yet, despite the weeks I spent talking about and preparing for their dying—and, in both cases, being with them at the end—there was much that remained fundamentally unknowable and mysterious when it finally happened. And so, the desire to understand, to *hold death in my hands*, persisted, leading me to spend several years writing a memoir about how their lives ended and what it meant to me.

As I turn my bike around and head for home, I pass yet another dead skunk. Unlike the earlier one that lay perfectly preserved on the side of the road, this one has suffered the full gory consequences of being struck by a passing car, and it's not a pretty sight. I have no desire to get closer to it. No impulse to touch or move it. But I do take a look as I ride by.

HAVE FUN AT THE FUNERAL, GIRLS

— *Sam Barry* —

Death. Talk about a punch line.

My father, David Barry, died at home. When good guys died in the movies, they always got in some great final lines or accomplished some final task that gave meaning to a sad moment. My dad's death, my first experience of a real human death, wasn't like that. There was no soft lens, no special music, no explanation of the meaning of life. Instead, we watched him slip further away into his memories. As the days and weeks passed, he spoke less and less, except to ask for chipped ice.

I remember sitting by his bedside, near the end. The Mondale/Reagan presidential debate was on TV.

"Who do you think won?" I asked him when the debate was over.

"The Cleveland Indians," he replied. I looked into his eyes. He wasn't joking. Dave had grown up in Cleveland, and I was pretty sure he thought he was somewhere back in the 1930s at this point. (The Cleveland Indians never won in the 1980s.)

Humor and laughter were an important part of our family life, and this held true as Dave lay dying. We laughed to relieve stress; we laughed in response to the absurdity of people offering pat answers to life's dilemmas; we laughed to ward off our fear; and we laughed at happy memories. Those last days were something of an extended wake, only the deceased wasn't yet deceased.

Years later, when I was a Presbyterian minister and required to represent a coherent belief system, I officiated at many funerals and memorials. I felt honored to do this work—when you are a pastor, you are invited (or stumble) into some very intimate territory. I also discovered that it was a good idea to lay aside preconceived notions of how others would behave or what people needed. Sometimes I encountered walls of anger, and it became clear that the home life of the deceased was not all love and roses. Other times people were manic and laughing, as if a party, rather than a death, were the matter at hand. Still others revealed no emotion; I might as well have been doing their taxes. When someone is dying or has died, expect every possible emotion: depression, relief, anger, giddiness, denial, happiness, sorrow, and yes, all possible forms of humor.

I remember presiding over the funeral of a motorcycle-riding poet and English teacher who had crashed on the highway and died. There was a big crowd, and I opened up the floor for anyone to share. Big mistake. It was like the funeral of Elvis, as woman after woman came up to talk about her passionate relationship with the deceased. It took me a few hours to regain control of the event.

Important as they are for the living, in some ways funerals and burials have very little to do with death, much as wedding planning and weddings have little to do with marriage. It's the mystery and finality of death that we live with in the dark night. Those who are left behind do most of their grieving alone, after everyone has gone home, in the months and years that follow. The reality of death is realized over time through thoughts, feelings, memories, discoveries, found and cherished objects, and all the ways in which a person is missed (or not) and remembered (or not).

My mother, Marion Virginia McAllister Barry, was fascinated by death. I suppose we all are, but Marion made a lifetime practice of thinking, talking, reading, and joking about death. I remember her reading *Enemy at the Gates: The Battle for Stalingrad*, by William Craig, a classic account of one of the most important and horrific battles of World War II, and excitedly telling me the details, such as how the residents of Stalingrad ate rats, shoes, or whatever to survive. These were my teenage years, and I was often stoned when she shared this information, so it made quite an impression on me.

Marion's interest in death and dying stretched back to her youth. She was raised in eastern Colorado and western Nebraska during the Dust Bowl era, a time and place that did not necessarily foster a cheery disposition. My grandfather was a mechanic who moved the family around, finding work in sugar beet factories and at one time trying his hand at homesteading. People often describe the great outdoors as wholesome, but a landscape littered with empty irrigation ditches ripe for a person to accidentally tumble into (this happened to Marion) and an atmosphere suggestive of the Apocalypse is probably not what they have in mind.

For a time the family lived in Minatare, outside of Scotts Bluff, in the Nebraska panhandle. Not much happened in Minatare, so Marion and her best friend Elizabeth had to find ways to entertain themselves. Once, when the two girls had been acting out in class, a teacher informed them that they were to stay after school.

With a broad smile on her face, Elizabeth turned to my mother and said, "Shall we, Marion?"

Because Minatare offered so little of what we normally think of as fun, the girls made do with whatever was happening in town. Sometimes this meant stretching the definition of entertainment to include funerals. Marion and Elizabeth would get in line to view the body, whether or not they had any connection to the deceased. One afternoon, as they were leaving the house, a neighbor stopped raking in his garden and said, in a droll Western accent, "Have fun at the funeral, girls."

Marion studied biology and English at the University of Nebraska at a time when the human race was locking onto the knowledge that germs are bad and cleanliness is good, and my mother took that message to heart. Between the dust that swirled everywhere and her newfound recognition of the omnipresence of germs, she developed an obsession with cleanliness. Her feeling was germs could kill and were going to get you eventually, but in the meantime we could stave off the Grim Reaper with copious amounts of bleach, ammonia, soap, and water, and by cooking the hell out of meat.

Marion's dark view was reinforced by world events: the Great Depression, which had hit the farmers all around the Dust Bowl years before, overtook the world, and then World

War II. She met my father and eventually moved to a suburb outside New York City, where my father, a Presbyterian minister, found work trying to cure the ills of the inner city, while my mother worked at being the perfect housewife, the postwar ideal for women.

Life was good in many ways. Armonk, New York, where they settled, was a lovely little town; they had four healthy children, a lovely, very clean home, enough money, and many good friends.

But happiness was for Marion a more ephemeral state than for most. She became moody enough that friends remarked on it; some even suggested solutions. Marion tried to tough it out. Unfortunately, she was trying to tough out clinical depression. Darkness settled over her spirit, and suicide began to look like a logical choice. Over the years she danced with the Grim Reaper, taking a few extra pills and knocking herself out for a weekend, edging ever closer to the negation of consciousness. And then she would return from the world of the dead, funny as ever. People were always delighted to see her. Wherever she went, people would shout her name, and she would respond with some edgy wisecrack or self-deprecating remark.

But there came a time when the depression that haunted Marion began to take over entirely. Dave was struggling with his own demons—alcohol and work addiction—and he was often away, and hardly there when he was present. Alone in the suburban wilderness, Marion began to slip deeper into her own hell of despair. Eventually, she reached the point where the oblivion of death seemed to be her only option, and one weekend, when no one was around, she took enough of those little pills to kill someone twice her size, washing them down with vodka for good measure. (Marion wasn't much of a drinker—that was Dave's department—so there was no question that the vodka was added for its medicinal effect.)

I was fifteen years old and a bit of a teenage hellion at the time, and was off on a weekend spree of partying that did not include checking in with my mother. However, I had a premonition that something was wrong and stopped at Hi Health, the local beer and cigarette stop, to use the pay phone and call home.

"Hi, Mom, I spent the night at Regis's," I said, referring to my partner in crime, Regis Goodwin. We could pretty much do whatever we wanted at the Goodwins' house—his mother worked the graveyard shift, and his dad pretended to maintain order as he watched Yankee games and got completely snookered.

"That's fine," she said, her voice flat and far away.

"Are you okay?"

"I'm fine."

There's fine, and then there's fine. Her voice, her responses, everything was a little off. The person I spoke to on the phone was like a hologram of my mother, not really there, slipping in and out of view. I made my decision. "I'm on my way home," I said, changing my plan, which was the standard plan for every night at that stage of my life: to find a party and meet the girl of my dreams.

I jogged the mile and a half home as fast as I could. The first thing I saw upon entering the house was a coffee cup on my mother's cherished oak dining table. An earthquake followed by a fire and a flood could have struck our town, and my mother would not have failed to put a coaster under a drink on that table. I walked in—slowing down, now, hesitating at the last moment—and there was her leg, sticking out at an odd angle on the floor. Her face was puffy. She was completely unconscious and did not respond to my calling to or shaking her. I saw the prescription bottles on the table.

I called the operator in a daze and was connected to the police; then I called my father, who was hours away in Manhattan and did not seem to fully grasp what I was saying. Then I stood outside the house and watched as the small caravan of emergency vehicles cruised down our peaceful, woodsy street. An ambulance and two police cars pulled into our driveway. One of the cops was joking about some vaguely crude matter as they entered the house. From the vantage point of decades later, I now realize that this was how he handled his job, which involved seeing much of the underbelly of humanity. I also realize now that he was a completely insensitive asshole.

The cop kept joking even after he saw the body, but it really didn't matter; it was all part of a strange, surreal play. Meanwhile, another officer took me aside and asked about my mother's medications. I showed him the drawer where she kept her prescriptions. Then they put my mother in the ambulance and drove away. The officer who asked about the drugs stopped and looked at me.

"You okay?"

"I'm fine." What else was I going to say? What do teenage boys always say? I sure as hell wasn't going to talk about any real emotions.

I wish I could tell you that it all ended happily, but we all know life doesn't end happily. The end is the end, and for the purposes of most storytelling it is quite unsatisfactory. The good news is that Marion recovered from that suicide attempt, though it was a close call, and then made great progress with a psychiatrist who treated her for depression. A year or so later, Dave came to terms with his alcoholism and never drank again. (I remained a hellion.) Dave and Marion had some good years together, but the toll of alcohol, overwork, and cigarettes eventually caught up with Dave and he died, too young.

After the funeral, Marion was walking back from Dave's gravesite accompanied by her four children and the family minister, when she stopped to read the name on a gravestone.

"So *that's* why I haven't seen him around," she said.

Marion always had her humor, but she couldn't accept growing old without Dave. She went into a tailspin a few years later, locked herself in a motel room, and took a boatload of pills. This time she succeeded in taking her own life.

I have a lovely picture on my bookshelf of my parents, Dave and Marion. A smiling Marion is looking at the camera, her arm around Dave's shoulder; he is laughing as hard as a person can laugh. It's easy to guess what's happened—Marion has made some outrageous, funny remark. She had that gift, and Dave appreciated it.

Yes, I remember them dying, but I remember them laughing, too.

DEATH WITH DIGNITY
— Sherry Glaser-Love —

After eight years in renal failure, combined with four-hour dialysis treatments three days a week, with a side of occasional Friday afternoon seizures that rendered her unconscious at the Cedars-Sinai bus stop, my mother has been deemed mentally competent by an ethics panel in a Los Angeles hospital to make the decision to refuse treatments, and therefore relinquish her life here on earth. She tells her frustrated little nephrologist that she wants one more dialysis treatment on Friday, so she'll be sure to live through the weekend. She wants to say her goodbyes. He reluctantly agrees and prophesizes that she'll panic and beg for dialysis on Monday.

We laugh at him.

She returns to her own room at the Garden of Palms assisted-living facility, and she is now under hospice care.

She has very little on her agenda. She needs to cancel her dental and chiropractic appointments. I sit on the bed next to her listening. They ask if she would like to reschedule. She says, "No, I'll be dead." There is a stunned silence on the other end. She thanks them for their time and hangs up. She then goes through her phone book calling long-distance relatives to tell them goodbye. Witnessing this is probably the most hilarious, terrible thing I've ever seen. Some fight with her, try to talk her out of it. Most cry out how much they love her and how much they are going to miss her. Before she hangs up, the last words are, "Remember, I love you, goodbye." With total consciousness, she is saying goodbye to her life here and eagerly anticipates leaping into my father's heavenly arms. She is ecstatic at the thought of their reunion. She shaves her legs. True love waits for her. That's heaven all right.

I watch my mother throw her bills into the recycling bin, try on coffin wear, and decide which shoes go with her eternal crepe turquoise dress. This seems like a good time to ask her if she'd like to say anything particular in her obituary. She pauses, looks heavenward, and says, "No matter how my life has been, I'm glad I had it."

I'm so happy for her. I'm so sad for me.

She's still taking excellent care of herself, taking all her medications and keeping to a proper renal diet. She says, "I want to look good and feel good when I die." But after eight years of a chocolate-free existence she has consented, with some coaxing from me, to have dessert every night. "That's the point, isn't it?" I tell her. "You need to live a little," so she does. The chef at Garden of Palms starts to cry from joy when we tell him she'll have dessert from now on.

After getting word of her imminent departure, three of our family clans gather on that very weekend to pay homage to my mother. She's having a going-away party.

On Sunday morning, we all meet at the French Market on Santa Monica Boulevard in Los Angeles. These are the kin my brother and I grew up with but haven't seen for a long time. Aunts, uncles, cousins, and such, everyone squeezing together in the restaurant's little centrally located indoor gazebo and ordering a lot of fried food and dips. And dessert, of course. It's like musical chairs up there. We all exchange seats to have a chance to visit the past, then we converge back at the Garden of Palms, where other residents are offended at the joy we share in just being together. One angry grandma says, "They have some nerve."

My generation and our kids sit in the umbrella shade of wrought-iron patio tables and listen well. We get to hear stories from the elders of the great migrations of our great-great-grandfather through Mongolia, and our great-great-grandmother's trek through Czechoslovakia with her six children. We tap the root. Together there are thirty of us, cross sections of three generations who have come to pay respect and gratitude to my mother, who over the last seventy years has brought us divine messages, manic comedy, true forgiveness, unconditional acceptance, and love, love, love.

So, in effect, she is orchestrating a ritual of death with dignity, compassion, and celebration. I hear the symphony. It is an extraordinary expedition into the complete unknown, trust, beauty, and surrender. I am not aware of any families that have had the privilege and good fortune to participate in a positive death experience, where one has the ability to have an intimate conversation with the dying—not fraught with suffering, misery, and fear but instead infused with liberation and exaltation.

Monday morning is more intimate. It is imperative that my mother have alone time with her sister, her nieces, my brother, and me. Door closed, sacred and divine apologies, confessions, forgiveness, and looking into the face of death, confrontation of immeasurable degree. Looking into the face of someone you've known your whole life, knowing they are going to die shortly and saying goodbye, is powerful with a capital P. My youngest cousin says goodbye to my mom in the dining room. She walks out and collapses in tears into my arms.

The family is departing in waves. By Monday afternoon, it is just me and my brother. I ask if there's anything she'd like to do. We agree that it's a relief that she doesn't have to be at dialysis. She says, "Let's go to the theater."

Two years earlier, my mother had gone around the block to the Lee Strasberg Theatre and submitted her play *Love as a Dying Art*. It is a black comedy about a middle-aged woman desperate for attention from her family, who pretends she is dying of cancer so they'll treat her with more love and respect. The receptionist had promised my mother that they would at least do a staged reading, so she could hear the play out loud. She was still waiting to hear it.

I say, "Great, let's go."

My brother says, "I'll drive her."

My mother says, "I want to walk."

I say to my brother, "I'll walk with her. What's the worst that could happen? She could die."

We laugh.

We leave the Garden of Palms and wobbly-walk about fifty yards to the corner, and then enter the theater. The woman at the desk recognizes my mother and begins apologizing, adding, "We haven't forgotten about you."

"Oh, I'm glad," says my mother, resting her arms on the counter. "I'm dying."

The lady goes pale. "Oh, I'm..."

"Well, I'd just like to hear my play before I die."

"Of course, I'm so sorry." She pulls out the calendar. "How's next Thursday?"

"No, I don't think so."

"Oh, ummm, how about this Thursday?"

My mother shakes her head.

"Maybe tomorrow."

"Oh, definitely," says Mom.

"Let me get your number, and I'll arrange it right away. I'll call you as soon as I get the actors together, and we'll do it in the little theater."

What an extraordinary feeling of revenge for all playwrights who have waited weeks, months, years, and sometimes forever to hear back!

By the time we return to Garden of Palms, it's time for dinner. Hamburger, zucchini, kugel, and chocolate cake for dessert. My mother is excited: everyone in the dining room is happy to see her. She has been a friend and kind angel to all of them. Some look confused because they know what's going on. Others are oblivious. I join her at the table with her best friends, Ruth, Phyllis, and Gloria. They know she's not long for this world, yet at the same time they are so excited that she is eating the same food as they are and that they can say "Isn't this delicious?" out loud. The chocolate cake tastes like it's been sweetened with Splenda, but they all like it very much.

It's seven o'clock. We go upstairs to her room. She conducts her nightly ritual: sponge bath, brushing her teeth, and flossing. Running around her room naked, she looks like a badly wounded little bird, with terrible bruises from the dialysis portals, flesh hanging where it used to be stuffed to the brim. She looks so fragile. It's hard for me to leave. I ask how she is.

She says, "I'm nervous."

I say, "What are you nervous about?"

She says, "Dying."

I ask, "Do you want to practice?"

"Yes."

We sit on the side of the bed where the oxygen tanks are set up. I take the tubes and place them gently around her head and place the hoses up her nose. "So, if you feel like you're dying, get into bed with these on, get comfortable, lie down, and relax. Breathe." She does a good job. "Either you'll fall asleep and wake up feeling better, or you'll die."

"Okay, that's easy."

We take off the apparatus.

She says, "I can't wait to see your father. I know he's waiting."

"Yes." I hold her hand. "I'm going to miss you so much."

"I know, my baby, I know. It's time for me to go."

I hug and kiss her goodnight. I ask if she's sure I should leave. She asks if I want to stay. I'm confused.

Earlier in the evening, the hospice nurse had taken her blood pressure, pulse, temperature. Normal. I thought: It's been a busy weekend with the whole family, I have quite a journey ahead, it could be a week or two before she goes, so I decide to head north on the 101, as opposed to the hotel, ten minutes away, to get some acupuncture and bodywork from my cousin Linda.

I tell her that I'll see her in the morning.

After my acupuncture treatment is over, I fall right asleep, only to wake up a little while later and wrestle with myself about getting up and going back to the hotel. But it is so warm and comfortable at my cousin's house, I can't even get my body to cooperate, so I surrender.

My mother wakes up at 5 AM, like she does every morning. She takes out her list of prayers from the bedside table, blessing us all and asking again for world peace. She takes her medication. She washes up and makes her bed. She falls. She gets up and gets dressed in a pretty aqua sweat suit, fixes her hair, and puts on her makeup. She goes to breakfast.

I wake up with a start and check my phone for messages. My mother has called at 9:09. I call her at 9:20, and she says, "I'm falling apart. I feel really cold. I walked down to breakfast, but I had to come back to my room in a wheelchair. I think you should come. I'm cold."

"I'll be right there. Is there anything I can bring you?"

"Chocolate."

I leap from the bed and am dressed in thirty seconds. I ask my cousin if she has any chocolate. She hands me a box of Dove chocolates in the shape of hearts. Perfect.

I get in the car and drive. My mother gets on the computer and makes a $10 donation to Doctors Without Borders.

I had such marvelous plans for my mother's final moments on earth. I had special music to die by. I intended to read the love letters written by my father to my mother when he was in the army for six months, before they were married. I had a stack of those and would use them to set the stage, the mood for their heavenly reunion. I had my yoga mat in tow and would stretch and breathe and use my physical body to release hers. Then I imagined, in the last minutes, I would crawl in her bed to be with her, take her in my arms, lay her head on my breast, and kiss her forehead until her last exhale.

But, as my great-grandfather used to say, man makes plans and God laughs.

So Tuesday morning, while I'm sitting in traffic on the 101, my mother dies. God must have gotten a real kick out of that.

I understood pretty quickly that I was where I was supposed to be. My brother was also in traffic at the time, and my sister-in-law, always at my mother's building, being the director of operations there, happened to be on the way to the dentist. It was Diane, a kind nurse who worked at Garden of Palms, who held my mother's hand as she took her final breaths. Just like we had practiced, Mom put on the oxygen, lay down, took three breaths, and then she died.

My mother's body is still warm when my brother and I arrive. We kiss and hug her one last time and cry a lot. While the man from the mortuary wheels her out on the gurney, the woman from the Strasberg Theatre calls.

"We have a cast ready for tomorrow evening."

"It's too late. My mother died this morning."

"Oh, I'm so sorry."

"Yes. I'm sure you are." Ah, the revenge of the playwrights.

According to the family psychic, Gloria, with whom Aunt Florrie has been consulting for the last thirty or so years, my father, in heaven, was standing in a circle with other family, and my mother surprised him. He knew she was coming, but it usually takes a week or so to get through purgatory and all the final arbitration of one's good and bad behavior. Yet my mother, pure of heart and soul, went VIP, express elevator, right to the pearly gates, where she was welcomed by archangels who recognized her as an old friend, and held open the gates as she waltzed right in.

According to the psychic, my father spun around, lifted her into his arms, and immediately drew the curtain. I guess they had some catching up to do.

Now, some of you might say, "Well, that's silly," or "How do you really know that happened?" I admit that it's challenging to trust. It requires faith. And we are filled with so much doubt, how can we trust that there is an afterlife, that it's good, that our dreams of heaven can be real? Well, as a family, we discussed this with my mom, and she agreed to send us a sign that in fact she was in heaven. This is just one of the blinding messages we got from the other side: My uncle, the family photographer and videographer, wanted to share some old movies with us after the funeral.

One of the tapes he pulled from his archive, which contained hundreds of hours of video, was a VHS tape my mother and father had recorded twenty years ago, as a birthday gift to her sister, Florrie, for her fiftieth birthday. The title of the tape was *Florrie Raises the Roof,* in which my mother parodied all the songs of *Fiddler on the Roof* and sang them as a tribute to my aunt. My mother crafted cardboard cutouts of the family, images that perfectly suggested our characters. There was a circle cut out for the faces, so my mother could stick her face into the hole and impersonate each of us, like my Uncle Paul singing, "Now I am a rich man, di di, did ididi dum." It was hilarious and very touching to see her portray us with such love and affection.

So what was the epiphany? It came with my mother's introduction to her production. The very first image we saw of her—and this was Saturday morning, after we buried her on Friday afternoon—was the beginning of the tape, in which my mother was dressed, as—a drumroll, please—a guardian angel. Yes, halo and all.

My mother's death was not traumatic; it was relaxing. She took the tragedy out of death—quite an accomplishment. She had no unfinished business, no loose ends. She went in peace. My mother put the wonder in wondrous, the marvel in marvelous, the truth in trust, the will in must. As our family tries to comprehend this *happy ending,* the ultimate oxymoron, we realize that each moment is precious, fragile, and more so because we witnessed her farewell to friends and family, in utter humility that serves us beyond measure.

She taught us how to die. A lesson that could, in a funny way, save our lives.

MY GRANDFATHER'S CHICKEN SOUP

— *Aviva Layton* —

It's amazing to me that, at the age of seventy-eight, I've seen a dead body only once.

I left Sydney at the age of twenty-one for Montreal, so when my parents, aunts, and uncles died it was always at a distance, few places being more geographically removed from the rest of the Western world than Australia. Close friends have died but, again, always at a remove. I've seen them sick and debilitated, but never actually dead. The only death I've ever witnessed was that of my maternal grandfather, Wolf Sniderman.

I can't say I loved my grandfather, but I was in awe of him and at times even feared him. He was a remote figure with whom I had no emotional connection whatsoever. Adding to this lack of connection was the fact that he spoke mainly Yiddish, his heavily accented English being the source of much embarrassment to me in 1930s Sydney.

My grandfather, having been told that his tubercular wife would not survive another winter, had left Lithuania with its harsh winters and harsher pogroms for the safety and sun of Australia, but it turned out to be too late to save her. She died shortly after arriving in Sydney, leaving behind a bewildered husband and four daughters stranded in an alien land. The sisters represented with almost mathematical precision—and in defiance of all fairy tales—descending degrees of beauty. That is, the eldest was the most gifted and beautiful, the youngest the least attractive and least talented, my mother being third in line.

All the daughters doted on their father, but my mother outdid them in her devotion to his every need and mood. I hadn't heard of Freud, let alone read him, but I always suspected there was something troubling about my mother's love for her father. It was as if she'd elected herself to be his surrogate wife. She used to tell the story of how, at the funeral of my grandmother, she had made him swear on his dead wife's body that he would never remarry. This story was a source of great pride to her. It's hard to imagine that Wolf Sniderman, this tall handsome man with his thick jet-black moustache and deep brown eyes, who was in the prime of his life, actually honored that awful promise. But he did.

The strongest images I have of my grandfather are on the occasion of the High Holidays when, with the rest of my family, I was forced to attend synagogue. I'd stare at him swaying back and forth, wrapped in a flowing blue-and-white *tallis*, looking like a vengeful ancient Hebrew prophet, and couldn't imagine how such a remote figure was related to me. It was the same at Passover, when he sat enthroned, presiding over the festive table that had been laid with care and reverence by his four daughters. There were bitter herbs, the burnt egg, the honey and apple, and the richly embroidered three-layered matzo cover that had been brought over from Lithuania along with the burnished gold candlesticks. A gleaming bowl with a fresh white monogrammed towel lay to one side of the throne, and an extra place was set for Elijah the Prophet, at whose place stood an elaborately chased silver goblet, also a relic from Lithuania.

I always dreaded Passover. As the youngest, I had to ask the Four Questions in Hebrew, and only if I recited them flawlessly would I earn a grandfatherly nod of approbation. But that wasn't the end of my fears. At some point in the evening, he would begin his darkly dramatic chanting of the Ten Plagues. For each one, we had to spill drops of red wine from our glasses, splotching the whiteness of our dinner plates as if they were gouts of blood. *"Dom ... Sfardayeh ... Kinim ... Arov,"* my grandfather would intone, until the last and most terrifying of all, the killing of the first-born *Makat b'choyroth* rolled off his patriarchal tongue like a stone.

Then arrived the moment I had been dreading the most—inviting the prophet Elijah to partake of our feast. To the adults, it may have been a symbolic act, but to me it was all too real. Somewhere out in that murky hallway which led to Grandpa's flat lurked some bearded hook-nosed old Hebrew who was even more intimidating than my grandfather. I was certain he was ravenous and vengeful at being kept waiting. Under his striped desert robes was hidden a sharp-bladed scimitar which I knew he would use on me, the nearest and most helpless prey.

In fear and trembling, I would open the front door and call out the words my grandfather had taught me to say, *"Eliahu*

Hanavi." No one answered, but I felt a hostile, alien presence in the shadows. My family, seated behind me, seemed millions of miles away. *"Eliahu,"* I whispered again, hoping he wouldn't hear me and, if he did, that he wouldn't accept the invitation. In all the years I had to do this, nobody ever answered, but I was always in a state of terror that someone with a heavily accented English like my grandfather's would one day call back to me through the shadows.

When he wasn't praying in the synagogue or presiding over the Passover table, Wolf Sniderman ran a small, dingy tailor shop in a rundown section of downtown Sydney. The Trouser King he called himself, and he had a huge sign outside his shop to back up his claim. He called me the Trouser Princess, and for years I really believed I was royalty. Somehow or other, the royal succession had skipped a generation, leaving my mother and aunts out of it altogether.

As a Trouser Princess, I was granted many privileges, my favorite being the privilege of looking at my grandfather's gold fob watch, which he wore in his waistcoat pocket. "It's a special watch," he'd say in his thick Yiddish accent. "It wears out by looking at it. Only to a Trouser Princess do I show it, and even then only for a second or two."

Despite his title, my grandfather was a very bad tailor. Worse, despite his last name of Sniderman, which means "tailor" in Yiddish, he was no tailor at all. The slacks he'd make me out of thick, dark, itchy remnants would always have one leg shorter than the other, the clumsily sewn crotch biting into my cleft until I felt as if I were being sawn in half.

The wonder was that my grandfather's shop flourished, but

it did, even though no Jew would be seen dead near the place. Only *shigotsim* flocked to the shop. "Id-yots," my grandfather called them, spitting out the last syllable as if it were a piece of undigested food. And idiots they must have been to tolerate my grandfather's insults and curses.

My mother often dropped me off at the store when she went shopping, and I'd cringe with shame when I heard a customer come into the shop for his first fitting. My grandfather, tape measure hanging around his neck like the professional he wasn't, would trot out some dusty old bolt of material and drape it around the poor victim.

It was in vain for the customer to protest that it wasn't even the color he'd initially selected, let alone the material. "Brown you want?" bellowed Grandpa. His voice rang with a fierce conviction. "Brown? With your coloring, your complexion? You want you should look like a mud pie? Like a lump of *sheis*?"

Shaking, I would cower under the wooden cutting table, waiting for the poor chump to crack my grandfather's jaw open with one heave of his tough *goy* fist, but there would always be a subservient silence. I never managed to figure out why. Was it because of my grandfather's towering presence? His bullying? His air of angry righteousness? Whatever the reason, when I mustered up enough courage to peek around the corner, there would be some shambling hulk, head hanging, feet shuffling, hands twisting in front of him.

While my grandfather's insults rained down on their heads, his customers would shuffle out, holding a clumsily wrapped package containing some butchered lump of material for which they had handed out part of their hard-earned pay. Or they would walk out with the suit on, hopping from leg to leg—I knew exactly how they felt—distorting their bodies to make up for the discrepancy in the arm length, the tightness across the shoulder, the crookedness of the seams, which even I could see were beginning to split open.

"Mr. Sniderman," one of them might dare to say. "Wouldn't you say there's a little shortness in one arm?" And here the poor man would apologetically extend one raw wrist that protruded a good three inches from an ill-made cuff.

"Id-yot!" my grandfather would yell. "Pull it down! Pull it! Can I help it if you stood like a crippled crab at the fitting? What do you want from me—my life? That I should spit blood? You want you should come in here with your *pishach* money and expect from me Savile Row? Leave already! Go! And next time you should want a suit, don't come to The Trouser King. Go instead to the pub, and drink your money away like the rest of your tribe!"

Why didn't the man whip out a pistol from his pocket and shoot my grandfather between the eyes? "Bang! Take that, you filthy Yid!" Or grab his arm and twist it right out of its socket. No. Instead, he stammered, apologized, and shuffled out the door sideways. And sure enough, when next he wanted a suit, he'd be back at The Trouser King, his head bowed low to receive his ill-fitting jacket and his portion of insults. What spell, I wondered, did my grandfather cast over his servile population? My belief in his royalty deepened. He was indeed a king and I his princess.

Then a terrible thing happened. Grandpa's brother, Louis Sniderman, opened a tailor shop less than two blocks from his brother's establishment. I guess he thought that sharing his brother's surname also qualified him to be a tailor. Not only that, but he decided also to call himself The Trouser King and hung a big sign out front to prove it. It was just like the fairy tales—the true king was the victim of his wicked brother's usurpation. But unlike the fairy tales, my grandfather didn't take sword in hand and do battle for his kingdom. Instead, he had an even larger sign erected that read "The Original Trouser King." Despite that, my belief in my imperial lineage began to wobble.

It finally shattered a year or two later when I was old enough to move around town by myself. I discovered that Sydney was infested with royalty. There was the Tie King, the Button King, the Umbrella King. My faith bit the dust. It became heartbreakingly clear to me that if my grandfather wasn't the Trouser King, then I wasn't the Trouser Princess. From that moment on, my grandfather ceased to hold much interest for me. And when, sensing this, he'd dangle his gold watch in front of my eyes, cajoling me to look at it as long as I wanted, I'd turn away in indifference.

When I was fourteen, my grandfather was diagnosed with terminal lung cancer. My mother fell into a deep depression and ignored everything else in her life—her child, her husband, her home, her friends—everything except the progression of my grandfather's disease. Despite his obviously rapid decline, she refused to accept the inevitable and stayed by his side day and night, insisting on feeding him the dishes he'd enjoyed all his life—gefilte fish, pickled herring, smoked roe, and, above all, chicken soup with noodles. Although he had long ceased to be the distant all-powerful figure of my childhood, it troubled me to see him in such a diminished state, pale and shrunken, his once flourishing moustache straggly and unkempt.

"Dad," my mother would plead when he tried to turn his mouth away from the offered dishes, "just one more mouthful. It's good for you. Just another bite."

Her three sisters, who took turns looking after their father, remonstrated with my mother to leave him in peace, but her insistence won out. She was a bully, my mother—not for nothing was she her father's daughter—and everyone, including my father and myself, was secretly afraid of her.

I deeply resented having to visit my grandfather. The last place in the world I wanted to be was in that hot, stuffy bedroom that reeked of sickness and stale air, but there were times, particularly on the weekends, when I couldn't avoid it.

One Saturday, a day when the mercury had climbed into the high nineties and I was looking forward to going to the beach with friends, my mother insisted I come with her. No amount of cajoling on my part would move her. Did she have a foreboding that this would be the last time either of us would see him alive?

Despite the sickening heat, my mother tried to persuade my frail and dying grandpa to eat up his steaming hot chicken soup. "Come on, Dad, it's good for you. Just a couple of mouthfuls. It'll make you feel better. One more spoonful, Dad. Just a little bit more."

Grandpa clamped his mouth shut and shook his head weakly.

"Just a sip, Dad. Just one sip of nice nourishing broth. Just one mouthful of *lokshen*."

My grandfather started to make ominous gurgling sounds and tried feebly to wave the soup away, but nothing could deflect his daughter from her self-appointed task.

I was sitting in a corner of the room reading *A New Girl at St. Chad's* by Angela Brazil, whose books about English boarding school adventures I adored. (I had already devoured *Five Jolly Schoolgirls* and *A Harum-Scarum Schoolgirl* and desperately wished my parents would send me away to a school like St. Chad's, where I could be jolly and harum-scarum and never have to cope with my family on a daily basis.) I was so immersed in the goings-on at St. Chad's that hardly anything could have induced me to take my eyes from the page, but my grandfather's obstinate refusal to give in to his daughter's bullying made me look over at him with admiration.

Suddenly, with a surprising show of strength, he pushed my mother out of the way and sat bolt upright. Opening his mouth wide, he spewed out a spongy mass of raspberry-pink tissue. It fell right into the plate of hot steaming chicken soup. Plop!

His eyes widened in surprise, and the last thing he saw before he died were the broken pieces of noodles splattered over the white sheet. For one horrible moment, I thought my mother would try to stuff the contents of both pink tissue and soup back into Grandpa's mouth, but then she dropped the bowl onto the floor and began to howl with disbelief and grief. I sat on my chair paralyzed with shock and stared at my grandfather's dead eyes.

My first thought was that my grandfather's watch had stopped dead in its tracks for good. My second thought was to wonder whether he knew that in the last moments of his life he had been part of a Jewish chicken soup joke.

As my mother continued to wail, I felt an insane bubble of laughter grow deep inside my gut. It grew larger and larger until it burst out of my mouth. I couldn't control myself. I howled and I rocked. I wet my pants. Tears rolled down my cheeks. The more my mother shrieked, the more I laughed until I thought I was going to pass out or else die for lack of breath. (I later found out that some people have actually died of laughter— a Greek comedy writer, Philemon, found one of his jokes so funny he died of a paroxysm of laughter and, in more recent times, a Danish man, Ole Bentzen, couldn't stop laughing while watching *A Fish Called Wanda* and died on the spot.)

Was my laughter caused by hysterics? By a deeply ingrained sense of the absurdity of life, which I seemed to have had since early childhood? It was probably a combination of the two, both of which had gotten me into deep trouble. All my life I'd been plagued by inappropriate laughter. One of the worst ordeals of my school days was Remembrance Day, when everybody had to close their eyes and think reverentially of the sacrifices made by "our boys." The solemn drone of Kipling's Recessional would fill me with a bleak foreboding:

Still stands Thine ancient sacrifice,
An humble and a contrite heart,
Lord God of Hosts be with us yet,
Lest we forget—lest we forget.

Who was this God of Hosts, and what exactly was I supposed never to forget? I was convinced, as usual, that everyone in the world knew except me. I didn't even know who "our boys" were, let alone the sacrifices they were supposed to have made. I thought they must have been vaguely related to Jesus, because I was always being told at school that He had also made sacrifices on my behalf, the significance of which also escaped me.

As soon as the two minutes of silence was announced, I'd look around surreptitiously. Everybody else's eyes were properly downcast, their faces obedient masks of sadness and sobriety. I had no doubts they were thinking the right and proper thoughts. The only infidel in the entire assembly was me. The Jewess. I knew with sinking certainty that my doom was sealed, that I was helpless to avert my fate. I was going to laugh. It would start off as a tiny trembling bubble, until it finally burst into a huge resounding yawp. I'd be sent to the principal's office and accused yet again of heartlessness, insensitivity, and callousness. After laughing hysterically all the way through my grandfather's funeral, that was exactly what my family accused me of too. Nor could I stop laughing at any further reference to my grandfather's death at family gatherings. I was a disgrace and a pariah.

Was it my grandfather's messy and undignified death that had made me laugh? A sort of payback for my childhood disenchantment, my precipitous fall from royal grace? I didn't know then, and I don't know now. I do know, however, that I still laugh at inappropriate moments. I giggled my way through my marriage ceremony and guffawed when I was sworn in as a Canadian, something that very nearly cost me my citizenship. The same thing happened when I became an American. I sometimes wonder whether I'll have both the wit and the will to laugh at the moment of my own demise. If I do, at least I won't be around to witness anyone else's anger at my offensive behavior.

I have only two regrets about that unforgettable incident at my grandfather's deathbed. One is that I wish I could have controlled myself in front of my mother; the other is that I wish I could say that to this day I can't bear the sight, the smell, or the taste of chicken noodle soup, but I can't.

I love it.

SHE LAUGHED UNTIL SHE DIED

— Victoria Zackheim —

Six weeks before she died, my mother and I were together in her apartment, a rare January sunlight streaming across the living room carpet and warming the sofa where she was nested. Aware that her life was coming to an end, Mom was becoming increasingly agitated. An avowed atheist, she was facing the reality—her reality—that there was no God, no life after death, no heavenly place awaiting her where she would be reunited with her husband and all those friends who had died before her. This could only mean that the end, the absolute and inarguable end of her life, was fast approaching.

She had been declaring for months that she was ready, that the quality and value of her life had run their course and that, had she the courage, she would bring closure to this *nonsense* herself. But she did not have the courage, perhaps not even the inclination, to end her life. So she lived on, her body failing her, her memory slipping, as she continued to be the victim of the cruelest trick of all: death was approaching, and she was poignantly and painfully aware of its proximity.

Mom was eighty-nine, a former art teacher, a painter, Scrabble demon, and political activist. She was a loving friend to her peers, an occasionally difficult and judgmental mother to her daughters. I recall many instances where I felt distrusted and disrespected, despite being a fairly serious girl and woman who followed the rules and rarely wavered from the path I was taught to follow.

When I was a teenager, she harped on the fact that I could get pregnant, like so many classmates, and bring shame to my life. I assured her often that I was innocent to the point of naïveté, yet she never wavered from her threats and accusations. When I was a middle-aged woman, she warned me about excessive spending, yet I was never in debt and so fiscally responsible that I too often denied myself the little luxuries I could afford. This difficult side of our relationship was heightened by my mother's stubborn nature, and compounded even more by a sense of entitlement that resulted in her often saying whatever she wanted, no matter the consequences.

Eighteen months before her death, there were signs of physical problems: general weakness, lack of appetite, blood pressure fluctuations. "I'm old," was her explanation whenever I pressed her to see her doctor. And then the falling, the 911 calls, my phone ringing at all hours to meet her at the hospital. Blood work, guesses, nothing firm. If I took a bath, the phone was perched on the nearby sink. If I ran downstairs to get the mail, the headset was grasped in my hand. I knew the call would come; I just didn't know when.

For the first time in their three-decade relationship, her doctor called me. "She's bleeding internally," said Dr. Candell. "I'm sure of it, but she refuses to have a colonoscopy." He asked me to help convince her, while he continued to plea and cajole. Meanwhile, she was slipping into a state of severe anemia, and a transfusion was given that alleviated her symptoms but did not stop her decline.

After several months and more emergency trips to the hospital, my patience was nearly gone. When next she was shuttled to the ER—I got that call at three o'clock in the morning—I raced across the Bay Bridge, surrounded by the eerie emptiness of a highway normally jammed.

Mom was so pale that she was gray. After the saline bag was empty and the transfusion was complete, I blocked the door of her examination room like some linebacker daring a runner to break through and announced that she was going nowhere until the colonoscopy was performed. With a dramatic scowl and teeth grinding, she begrudgingly agreed.

Instead of the two hours it normally takes to drink the bowel-cleansing solution, Mom drank hers in forty-eight. That was my mother. Heels. Dug. In.

Finally prepped for the procedure—a euphemism for having everything cleaned out and the entire colon visible through an intestine-traveling camera—she was transferred to a gurney and wheeled into the examination room. I waited outside, concerned that this invasive but rarely dangerous procedure might be too much for her. In less than an hour, the doctor joined me.

Colon cancer.

Nearly total blockage.

Laparoscopic surgery would do the trick, probably cure it. He doubted there would be a need for radiation or chemotherapy.

I called Dr. Candell and asked him to come and talk to us. We needed his expertise, his calm nature, to guide us through what would be the most important decision of my mother's life. Most of all, we were desperate to hear the opinion of a medic who truly cared about her well-being and, more importantly, her quality of life.

Within a few hours, he was sitting in her hospital room, holding her hand and quietly going over her options. There were two: surgery and hospice. He confirmed what we both suspected, that any surgery performed on a woman nearing ninety had its risks. And not so much the surgery itself—hers would be less invasive than many—but the damage that the anesthesia could cause to her organs and her level of strength. What frightened us was the knowledge that anesthesia can cause long-term cognitive disorder, especially in the elderly. Was it worth the chance, subjecting my sharp-minded, opinionated, and creative mother to this risk? What if she came out of the surgery cancer-free, but with short-term, and even long-term anesthesia-induced senile dementia?

"How long will I live if I choose hospice?" she asked.

The doctor's eyes softened, his fondness for my mother evident. "Three to six weeks."

She chose hospice.

I phoned my children and then my sister. As the firstborn, Michele had taken the brunt of our mother's nasty tongue. This was compounded by the fact she is a gifted and recognized artist and writer, and our mother long envied her daughter's accomplishments. That envy manifested itself as an undercurrent of ill-treatment from a woman who had aspired to similar recognition.

Like so many women of her generation—especially highly intelligent and creative women—Mom lacked the ability to take risks. While she insisted that her life had been fulfilling, there was a bitterness that ran through her relationships with her children. When learning of our mother's decision to choose death over surgery, Michele would have been more than justified in distancing herself. Instead, she assured me that she would fly in immediately. With our mother only days from hospice, it was a relief to know that Michele would be there to support her—and in so many ways, me—through this process of dying.

The day of the colonoscopy, shortly after Dr. Candell took his leave, a surgeon showed up in Mom's room. The hospital had contacted him prior to her decision, so he arrived with no knowledge that she had chosen death over surgery. He was young, attractive, and friendly. I assumed that surgeons in his age group would be more supportive of life/death choices, so I was comforted by his presence.

Mom informed him that she was going into hospice. "I'm old, I'm tired, and I prefer a quiet and pain-free death," she explained.

The surgeon nodded thoughtfully, which allowed me to think: enlightened generation, accepting and respectful of personal choice. He stood at the foot of her bed and leaned against the railing. His face radiated concern and comprehension. And then he spoke. "Your death will be anything but quiet and painless," he said. When I asked him to explain, he looked directly at my mother. "You'll stop eating, but there will be times when you'll want a little something. With this blockage, you'll soon be vomiting your own feces."

My mother's eyes widened until they bulged. I had seen fear in her face many times—going back to when I was a teenager and she suffered from an autoimmune disease that had taken her near death on several occasions—but I don't recall ever having seen that look of terror. Had I not been caught off-balance by this man's insensitive declaration, I would have challenged him. I would have asked, With morphine helping her into a coma, why would she eat? I would have asked, And if she did eat, wouldn't it be sips of water and juice? Instead, I sat there stunned by the vile picture he had created...and then it was too late. My mother had already visualized, with an imagination that comes from sixty years of painting, a tableau that was as inhumane as it was revolting.

The next day, she underwent surgery.

She bounced back physically, but something was amiss.

This woman whose mind had always been sharp and probing was struggling to remember the simplest things. And she knew it.

There were days when she asked me the same question four times ... in a period of five minutes. There were moments when she stared at me, yet had just enough awareness not to ask who I was or what the hell I was doing in her bedroom.

The delirium of anesthesia, compounded by the extended anemia—which could have been avoided, had she allowed simple tests to be run early in her illness—resulted in an increasing dementia that became part of her daily life.

"She'll come out of it," said her friends. And it was true, there were hours at a time, often days, when her mind seemed clear and she understood everything going on around her, including the political discussions on C-SPAN. On those days, my heart soared with the possibility that she was coming back.

But more than the occasional rallies were the signs that she needed increased care. The cancer was gone—and with it, the blockage—but she had little appetite and she was severely depressed. I suspected that she wasn't taking her medications, so I kept a tally of how many there were on a given day and compared those numbers to what remained in the bottles three days later. She was missing six pills for blood pressure, when only three should have been taken. The thyroid pill count had not changed. As for the vitamins, minerals, antidepressants, pain pills, and sleeping pills, the numbers were all over the place.

Several years before her illness, Mom had sold her town house and moved into a retirement community for seniors who enjoyed independent living. Despite the number of elderly residents pushing walkers and an average age hovering near eighty, I'd never seen such comings and goings! There were poker games, movies in the leather-seated theater, Democratic club meetings and residents' committees that, urged on by my leftie mother, might have threatened to build barricades and storm the management offices if demands were not met.

There were lectures and concerts, van rides into San Francisco for museum and gallery tours, dances, and mah-jongg games.

Fortunately for my mother, Cardinal Point was also a haven, an elegant and comfortable place that rivaled many four-star hotels, and was staffed by the kind of people anyone would choose to watch over their aging parents. One of their services was to provide daily care for residents recovering from illness. If able, they could remain in their apartments and be visited several times a day by aides. For Mom, this was a blessing. Morning and night, someone was there to be sure she was comfortable, that the correct medications were being taken, and that I had everything I needed to care for her. I continued my morning-to-night visits, but I also welcomed and appreciated the support. As someone who occasionally is tripped up by her own hubris, I found it difficult to let go of control. But as incontinence became an issue, I soon learned to ask for help.

One afternoon, we were together in her living room, Mom nested on the sofa as she attempted to concentrate on her crossword puzzle. Quietly, she put down the paper and turned to me. "I believe in the Eskimo tradition," she said. "I'm going to die soon. Why can't you just take me to Alaska and put me on a block of ice and float me out to sea?"

At first, I wasn't sure how to react, but then something struck me. Taking this as one of those moments when levity might be appreciated, I said, "Well, with global warming, I'm not sure there's much ice left."

She stared at me for a moment. "If there's no damned ice," she responded, "just hold my head underwater!"

And then we laughed. It was one of those wonderful, belly-shaking laughs that makes you feel joyful and reminds you that life is worth living. It was also the perfect entrée into a discussion about how she wanted to die, and what she wanted after death, in terms of burial or cremation, funeral or memorial service. One little laugh together became an important segue: now I knew her final wishes.

Within a few months, the aides were checking in every hour. Several times a day, I had to call them to help clean Mom and change her bedding. There was a commode next to her bed, which she hated. Looking back, I realize how quickly she went from expressing her distaste of that commode to an unawareness of its presence. I wonder if placing the commode nearby—an object she found undignified and distasteful—in some way hastened her desire to die.

I walked in one morning and found Mom chatting with one of her friends, a neighbor who had dropped by to bring her some breakfast. She had stopped eating several days earlier and we were all working together—friends, family, aides, anyone—to urge her to eat. I was delighted to see that Mom was nibbling on toast and that there was color in her cheeks. "You're looking better today," I declared.

"You know, I'm feeling better," she responded, with a lilt in her voice I hadn't heard for months.

I looked at her and smiled. "That's too bad," I told her, "because I need a new car."

Her friend was shocked, perhaps even offended.

Mom and I shared a laugh. She had mentioned on many

occasions how her estate would provide a little financial cushion for me. A few times, after she offered to buy me a new car, which I didn't need, I told her I'd wait until she died and splurge on something totally outrageous: low, fast, expensive.

As we became more comfortable with the subject of her death, I asked about her childhood in Manhattan, the acting classes with Lee Strasberg, the camp her father ran where only Yiddish was spoken and where she met my father, and memories of her marriage, motherhood, and her career as a teacher and artist. During these conversations, and often supported by anecdotes that included humor (forced or otherwise), we were able to slide quietly into discussions about our relationship, including the difficult times and wounded feelings; the pain I carried from a childhood passed with little mothering—at least, the affectionate, kisses-smothering kind—and her regrets at not having been a loving, supportive mother throughout my childhood and a good part of my adulthood.

I thought it odd at the time, but I now realize that it was because of the inherent power of humor that we were able not only to laugh together but to use that levity as a way to reveal to each other where our relationship had gone wrong. Humor softened the anger, opening a door that allowed us to step through and repair some of the damage.

While we could laugh about some things, other areas tested our patience. Mom thought I was bossy and too quick to make decisions for her. I became annoyed with her unwillingness to allow little if any wiggle room for beliefs that diverged from her own. Art, books, philosophy—you name it. But nothing brought out the claws faster than religion.

She was not a wavering atheist whose beliefs might be jarred with one good miracle, but one of those "there is no God, no heaven and no hell" atheists. In truth, she fit very nicely into that group of "don't give me that religion crap" atheists who denigrate anyone who dares to question the existence of a divine presence. As she moved closer to death, an interesting thing began to happen. No, my mother did not discover God. What she did discover, however, was that her belief that she would die and that would be that—forget heaven, hooking up with old friends, running into your deceased husband—unsettled her. No second chances to come back and do it right; no reincarnations to be the woman she perhaps wanted to be, which was a risk-taker and adventurer. I saw it in her face when she talked about death. Fear. Finality. Period.

It may have been my recognition of her fear of death that led me to humor, as well as my sometimes inept attempts at jollying her out of the doldrums of dying, but humor became a means to fix our damaged relationship. And then it became an energy that ran between us and allowed us to breach a wall built on more than sixty years of distrust. Humor was our shared gift. For me—and I believe for my mother as well—humor not only provided a measure of respite from the sheer pain of her illness, but eased the emotional and physical tension that comes with illness and dying.

The day I arrived and found my mother snuggled on her sofa and watching not C-SPAN but a children's cartoon, I knew that she was near the end of her life. "What are you watching?" I asked, and she responded, her speech labored and her voice low, "I have no idea."

The following week, my sister arrived. Six days after that, Mom died.

TRAGEDY PLUS TIME

— *Christine Kehl O'Hagan* —

On his deathbed, Morris Zelig tells his son that his life is a meaningless nightmare of suffering, and the only advice he gives him is to save string.

—WOODY ALLEN, *ZELIG*

Deathbed is such a quaint word, on par with *spats, antimacassar,* or *chifforobe.* You never hear of deathbeds that are posture-pedic, or sofa-bed deathbeds, or death-bunk-beds (unless, of course, you fall from the top of one). I have never seen a deathbed futon. There are no inflatable death mattresses in the LL Bean catalog, although maybe there should be, as a warning to those intrepid campers who might otherwise become s'mores for grizzlies.

There are, however, certain people who like the word *deathbed* and the attention it garners. Call her Molly. (Not so much because Ishmael was already taken, but because that was her name.)

Molly was my old friend Theresa's aunt (all names other than Molly's are pseudonyms), and although this is a true story, some of the details are, as the writer David Sedaris puts it, "true-ish."

Molly was a dissatisfied, unpleasant ninety-year-old lady who lived in the Forest Overlook Care Center. (This is not only a pseudonym but also a misnomer, for the only "forest" the place "overlooked" was a single mimosa tree set into an artificial red-brick island in the middle of Queens Boulevard, and the "care" there was iffy.)

Though Molly had been at Forest Overlook for ten years, she joined in no activities, neither arts and crafts nor Ice Cream Sundaes nor Friday at the Flicks, not even when Tammy, the recreation director, managed to score some black-and-white 1940s classics, a time when (most of the residents agreed) movies told stories without all the shootings, cursing, and sex, all of that baloney garbage you get today.

According to Mrs. Feinberg, the Forest Overlook social worker (who rarely called Theresa, the oldest, most responsible niece, to complain about her aunt), Molly even ignored warmhearted Father Joe, a priest and guitarist, whom everyone at Forest Overlook adored. Father Joe, who had a standing Saturday afternoon gig in the Forest Overlook rec room, where he stood underneath the *Sound of Music* mural and played every single request. (Theresa had seen that mural once. A young art student from Queens High School had painted it, and somehow Maria Von Trapp, trapped on that wall in a weird, open-mouthed position, looked like Ozzy Osbourne.) Mrs. Feinberg said that Molly was the only resident who never came to the rec room to see Father Joe, even though week after week, before he left, Father Joe made it a point to stick his head into the doorway of Molly's room and smile hello. "He smiles," Mrs. Feinberg told Theresa, but Molly scowls and gives Father Joe—the sainted Father Joe—what he himself calls "the evil stink eye."

Theresa didn't know what to say, other than "Aunt Molly's always been difficult."

"*Duh*," whispered Mrs. Feinberg, but Theresa heard her anyway and ignored it.

For entertainment, Molly watched ancient game shows (hosted by old TV personalities with terrible toupees) on the small set on her nightstand, did word puzzles, rewrote her will, and when she was bored with those things, insisted that the staff move her to another room. Each of Molly's rooms (some of which she had lived in a half dozen times before) had a shelf life of about two months, and then Molly began complaining. The rooms were either too hot or too cold, or her roommates snored or the sitcoms they watched were idiotic, or their visitors were rude, loud, inconsiderate, and smelled of foreign food. She complained that she was too close to the elevator, or too close to the kitchen where the smell of normal American food ("such as it is in this place," Molly said) made her sick.

It was easier for the staff to shift Molly from one floor to another, from one room to another, than listen to her complaints. The staff knew that the only time Molly's mouth was still was when the rest of her was in motion.

Though Molly had never been married nor had any children of her own (which was just as well, since she was one of those all-too-common adults whose interest in children was mainly punitive), she did have Theresa and Theresa's four sisters, five nieces in all, the sweet Sweeney girls. Unfortunately, on the rare times that they were all together, Molly liked to remind the girls of their terrible past haircuts, misspent youths, their wild, old, wanton ways, then she segued into their present polyester clothes, the cheap shoes on their feet, their spoiled children, and their poor taste in husbands, all of whom she'd described, at one time or another, as "the dumbest man on God's green earth."

Molly's nieces, sweet as they were, hated her, and who would blame them?

Why, even their late mother, the semibeatified, compassionate, tolerant, loving pillar of the church, Margaret Sweeney, had hated Molly too.

(On the morning after Bill Sweeney's funeral, Margaret Sweeney, wearing a green chenille robe whose pockets bulged with sodden tissues, got out of bed, staggered into the kitchen, and picked up a Mass card someone had left on the counter. When she saw Molly's signature scrawled across the bottom, she tore the Mass card in half and stuffed it into the garbage. "At least we're done with that son of a bitch," Margaret said, ignoring the shocked expressions of her five daughters who were sitting around the table amidst the unopened fruit baskets, methodically plowing their way through a pink box filled with fresh donuts, their elbows stuck to the plastic tablecloth with confectioner's sugar.)

One winter afternoon, from her current room at the Forest Overlook, Molly called Theresa and complained (in what Theresa thought was the world's most irritating voice) that she hadn't seen any of her nieces for years, that their father,

her only brother, Bill, would be ashamed of all of them, that ignoring their aunt was a form of elder abuse, especially now that she was ninety years old and also on her deathbed.

Theresa, the fair, sympathetic person she is, felt guilty.

"Sometimes, the residents know more than we realize," Mrs. Feinberg told Theresa when she called. "If your aunt says she's dying, well, she just might be right."

The next day, Theresa forced herself and cajoled her four sisters into leaving their twelve collective unbathed children home on Long Island in the care of those "dumb" but tired husbands, with all of their kitchen tables covered with smudged ditto sheets filled with half-assed homework. She picked everyone up, and they headed off to Queens. It was a freezing weeknight, and the sisters, except for Theresa, were drowsy and half asleep, until Exit 41N when their Dodge Caravan hit a patch of ice and for a few sickening seconds slid sideways. Then everyone sat up and suddenly came alive, an angry nest of buzzing hornets. Why were they doing this? they asked each other (while Theresa held onto the steering wheel with white knuckles). Daddy was dead, for Christ's sake, and here they were, mothers with children, risking life and limb for the old bitch whom they hated beyond belief. She was going to hell anyway, and this was the last time they'd see her, dead or alive, since none of them was going to her wake. As far as any of them cared, they yelled (except Theresa, who had noticed a bus behind her and had started praying), "Mrs. Feinberg could stick Aunt Molly into a black Hefty bag and drag her to the curb." If they got home alive, the younger girls said, and Theresa wanted to see

Aunt Molly ever again, she'd have to go by herself. The rest of them were O-U-T.

"Whatever," said Theresa, praying to St. Christopher, who was now discredited, and therefore a little bit useless.

Five angry freckled faces trudged through the heavy Forest Overlook front door and into the vestibule. The sisters stepped on the Oriental rug cemented to the nonstick tile floor, past the brass flowerpot (overflowing with plastic, variegated philodendron) on the tiny cherry table, then into a lobby filled with little loveseats, all covered like matching doll furniture in the same little burgundy and navy blue itty-bitty flower print, then shrinkwrapped, somehow, in waterproof, non-glare plastic.

Into the elevator and off, down the hall the sisters went, skirting the old people double-parked in wheelchairs outside their rooms, past the empty rec room where the TV blared with ads for hair dye and frozen pizza (frantically devoured by ecstatic families gathered around banquet-sized tables in palatial kitchens).

Five sisters, even Theresa, one common thought: Freaking old freaking fuck-face Aunt Molly.

But everything changed when they got to the door of Aunt Molly's room and found themselves face-to-face not with Aunt Molly's cranky, scowling northern end, but her in-your-face and very naked southern end. The poor thing! they thought, seized with pity for the poor old woman with her nightgown up around her waist, her shrunken legs kicking like a Rockette, her nether parts not only shockingly bald but also very crumpled-up, looking for all the world like something that forgot to put in its teeth.

Aghast by what was before their eyes, for the Sweeney sisters were good Irish Catholic girls who had never seen such an expanse of "out-there" womanhood, not even their own (although they came of age in the feminist 1970s, not one of them had ever bought so much as a speculum), the girls rushed to the old lady's bed so fast that they bunched up in the doorway and when they got free, Amy, the youngest, was sent flying halfway across the room.

They were in such a semihysterical frenzy to get to those blankets at the foot of Aunt Molly's bed, restore her dignity by covering up, if not the Sweeney family jewels, then surely the Sweeney family purse, that they forgot to look at her face.

Until Amy, who'd walked to the head of the bed, shrieked, "This isn't Aunt Molly!"

At that moment, Aunt Molly was in the room across the hall, propped up in what would be (five years later) her death-bed, but in the meantime, there she was, surrounded by puzzle books, watching a thirty-year-old rerun of *Family Feud* and cutting all of them out of the will.

So the Grim Reaper walks into a bar and orders a beer and a mop.

Listen up, Grim Reaper. If everything goes okay, I have about twenty years before you and I hook up, and I've got to tell you that, so far, you've taken too many in my family, and now you're starting in on my friends. I mean, plucking my son Jamie out of our lives was one thing, those first few years when I felt as though my body were turned inside out, and then dragged through gravel, and then there was my nephew and those two premature grandsons I never got to know. That was bad enough, but now Paula, my neighbor and friend of thirty-one years—well, she's gone too. For thirty-one years, through all of those seasons, she stood at her kitchen window and I stood in my yard, where (over the fence and through the thicket of trees) we talked each other's ears off and laughed ourselves sick. We'd had so much history. City girls, the two of us, not yet thirty years old when we first met, she was from Brooklyn and I was from Queens, and neither one of us was crazy about the flora and fauna of living in the sticks. Our mothers (her Italian Rosie, someone who claimed to have once danced in Atlantic City with Bert Parks, and mine, the Irish Helen, who claimed to have once had a conversation with Jackie Gleason in Bickford's Cafeteria, improbable as that might sound, with all the time Jackie Gleason had spent in Toots Shor's) were each a handful.

Paula and I raised rambunctious children; both of us buried sons.

Paula and I laughed about the day my older son took the bag of garbage instead of his lunch to school and the time that he suction-cupped Christmas ornaments to his forehead and couldn't get them off.

We laughed about the day I saw the red-jacketed prowler in the yard, and Paula chased him through the woods with the fireplace poker. With Paula's kitchen window closed and the blinds so tightly drawn, things are so quiet.

I'm old enough, Mr. Grim Reaper, sir, to see you all over the place. You're everywhere I look, breathing down a neck, sitting on a shoulder, up to your eyeballs (if you even *have* eyeballs) in mankind, humanity's constant companion, the companion everyone hates. You have no social skills; you tell no jokes. (Something tells me that humor is not exactly your forte, but don't give up hope. In another million or so years, maybe you'll become funny. As Alan Alda's character, Lester, said in Woody Allen's movie *Crimes and Misdemeanors,* "Comedy is just tragedy plus time.") I don't think you can sing or dance. Except for the overdosed quarterback here, and the reckless pitcher in the Porsche there, you don't seem to favor any one sport, nor follow any particular team. When you're out there picking and choosing, one self-destructive athlete is as good as another.

No one ever invites you to get-togethers. Can you blame them? Imagine yourself walking through someone's living room. All of that shrieking and yelling and guests all over the place, plastered to the walls, jumping through the windows. What fun would that be for you, standing there all alone, hanging off the mantle?

No one ever invites you to dinner. Can't you take a hint? Where would the host or hostess seat you? The minute you sat down, why, everyone else would run out of the room—half a dozen people stomped on and crushed. (You'd get a hernia dragging home—wherever your home *is* exactly—all that fresh meat.) Not to mention the empty chairs and that nightmare of leftovers.

And speaking of a host or hostess—who would want to greet you at the door, take your scythe and stick it in the umbrella stand, take your long black hoodie and lay it across the bed?

Who wants to know if the Grim Reaper goes commando?

Nobody invites you along on vacation. The Grim Reaper on a cruise ship—well, it just wouldn't work. The minute you entered the dining room—first seating, second seating, it wouldn't matter—everyone jumping out of their seat, huddling on the other side of the boat, and before you know it, the whole shebang is on its side, and there's Shelley Winters swimming past the porthole.

I don't go to the gym, but I do read the papers, and it seems you sometimes stalk around weight rooms, waiting for those out-of-shape middle-aged men to bench press 350 pounds. It wouldn't surprise me to learn that you've been spotted at the all-you-can-eat Chinese buffet, licking your well-concealed lips at the fat people walking around with those plates piled high with shrimp toast and crab rangoon.

(Sometimes, I sense you following me through the mall, and from all the frantic shopping all around me—well, I'm not the only one who feels that way.)

You're getting old now, Grim—happens to the best of us. After a million or so years in the same line of work, with no hope of either advancement or retirement (no Arnold Palmer Retirement Village for you and certainly no gold watch: you have neither golf pants nor wrists), even a Reaper like yourself starts to slow down. It's not like the good old days, with all of those plagues, the oozing, the bleeding, the pustules (I'll bet you haven't seen a good-sized pustule since the last hoarfrost). With people living longer, you've got no job security. The handwriting is on that wall. (Have you considered a second job? Working extra days and nights? Graveyard shift?)

From what I can see, you're not exactly the sharpest crayon

in the box. You don't seem to understand that you should leave the babies and young people alone and instead take only those who are very, very old, the ones being chased down eternity's corridors by far too many machines.

Not to be negative, but I think you're very rude. You plucked my nephew from this life before he'd finished his one last poem. You took my little grandsons much too early, just grabbed them from their mother's womb. You didn't have permission to take my son from that hospital bed, and neither did you ask Paula before taking her baby from that bassinet. (I'd like to think of all of those boys together, in some field-of-dreams stadium, my mother, Helen, and Paula's mother, Rosie, sitting together in the stands, watching all of those boys playing the baseball games they were denied in life, cheering them on in those cigarette-roughened voices.)

I know, of course, that none of this is your fault, and that "kill the messenger" is not a literal statement, no matter how tempting the idea. After all, you, too, answer to a higher authority.

Even if it was advertent, there were things you left behind. Not a hat, not an umbrella (not a hoodie, not a scythe), but memories. Not so much in the scheme of things, I suppose, but they're mine to keep, and I'll take what I can get. My nephew, sitting in front of me in his wheelchair, arguing with me about the existence of God (by now, he knows who was right), and then there was my second premature grandson, the one I got to hold, the one whose forehead I got to kiss.

There's my last memory of my son, when the *him* of him was gone and his dear body looked like driftwood lying there in that hospital bed, pure, white, beautiful, as though whittled out of birch or ash.

Then there's Paula, lit up in that kitchen window for all eternity, with all the laughter that passed between us snagged like webbing somewhere on that fence, or somewhere in the ivy that's wrapped around the trees.

> Murphy, O'Brien, and Kelly are in a Dublin pub, hoisting a few, when the talk turns to wakes, and what they'd like people standing over their caskets to say about them. "I'd like people to say that I was a hard worker and took good care of my family," said Murphy. "I'd like people to say that I was an upstanding member of the community and I took good care of my mother," said O'Brien. Then it was Kelly's turn. "I'd like people to say, 'Would ye look at that? He's moving!'"

When my eighty-year-old mother-in-law, a "gambling granny," fell and broke her hip, we thought she was a goner. We should have known better. She had surgery, pins in her hip, and she recovered. Then she fell again, and broke her other hip. She had more surgery, more pins, laughing along with us at our lame "Bionic Nana" jokes, and again she recovered. Then she fell and broke her shoulder. No surgery, no pins this time, yet she recovered. Then she fell again, and this time it was the "mother lode," so to speak, of Mom's injuries. She fractured her skull.

When we went to see her, half of her face was exactly the same as ever, but the other half was black and purple, swollen as an eggplant. Her cheeks, pressed to mine, had always felt soft as an antique linen tablecloth, but after the fractured skull, her face looked as pitted as an orange peel and somewhat leathery. I looked into her soft, dark eyes, trying not to cry. Mom hadn't seen her own face at all, and didn't know how bad she looked. "You should see the other guy," she said, and instead of crying, relieved at how much herself she seemed, we laughed.

Because nobody had told us anything different, we figured Mom was doing fine, but she was in an overwhelmed, understaffed city hospital where nobody explained to us that in a head injury, especially in an old person, the damage is not always immediate, that bleeding takes a while to spread throughout the skull, and sometimes the full damage takes a while to assess. We thought the fractured skull would be like the other injuries, that she would heal and be back to herself, but that didn't happen.

When she was in the hospital, Mom was that familiar self for only a short time, and then, suddenly, she wouldn't open her eyes, and she fell into a state of shuddering and continual yawning, in and out of something resembling sleep. It was as if one day my husband, Patrick, was helping her unwrap the saltines on her dinner tray, and the next day he was spoon-feeding her, and the day after that, the tray sat untouched in front of her, and she was unresponsive. We were bewildered, not knowing if Mom heard or understood anything we said to her. It didn't look good.

One afternoon, when Patrick went off to look for the doctor, I took matters into my own hands, so to speak. Standing by the side of the bed, I rubbed her arm. She had been a good mother-in-law to me, and I loved her. I took her hand, a miniature version of her son's, and held it softly. "It's okay to let go," I told her, "we'll be okay. Just go to the light."

At that moment, her eyelids flew open and she looked at me with something like shock, and for a minute I felt like a Judas. (True, I'd always had my eye on her Depression-era, cranberry-glass candy dish, but I could wait.)

"What light?" she asked me. "I'm going to Atlantic City!"

She never got there of course, but her skull healed, and she went back to her apartment, where she became someone like her former self, only newly assertive: a Nana who called Life Alert when she couldn't close her bedroom window, a Nana who called the fire department when she wanted to watch Channel 2 and had lost the remote controller in the bedcovers, a Nana who then called the mayor's office to complain about the racket and the mess the firemen made when they came with their axes and broke down her front door.

> *In summing up, I wish I had some kind of affirmative message to leave you with. I don't. Would you take two negative messages?*
>
> —WOODY ALLEN

I COULD DIE LAUGHING

— *Leon Whiteson* —

My granduncle Solomon played a dual role in my hometown in Southern Rhodesia in the 1950s—as the local Jewish community's official *shokhet*, or kosher slaughterer, and its unofficial sardonic jokester. These twin talents often ran together, as in: "Do you know the hens make this funny cackle when I slit their gullets? Like they're literally laughing their heads off at some private joke at our expense." He claimed that when he'd killed his last fowl, he'd slit his own throat and laugh his head off at "the biggest joke of all, my life."

The joke life played on Uncle Sol began at birth, back in the Ukrainian shtetl that was the family's ancestral village. Apparently, he was a fraternal twin. His mother had already delivered five boys, and she desperately wanted a girl. However, Sol's twin sister was stillborn and he survived, much to his mother's chagrin. In revenge, she saddled him with the pet name of *krumeh oigen* (cross-eyed), though this affliction was barely noticeable. In the family, he was known simply as Krumele. As my mom said, Sol was *krume*, "and not only in his *oigen*." Perhaps it was this cursed epithet that caused him to be a lifelong bachelor—that, along with his often thoroughly nasty but sometimes hilariously bitter tongue. The nickname he chose for me was "Boots," suggesting I was way too big for them altogether. This irritatingly apt tag stuck for years while I was growing up.

From the time I was eight, I was given the task of accompanying our African cook, Sout, when he took the Sabbath chickens to Sol's shed on Friday afternoons. My mother insisted I go along because the *schwartzes* (blacks) could not be trusted; she said they'd vanish for hours to "whoop it up with their pals at the drop of a hat."

The shokhet shed was a veritable poultry Auschwitz, a hellhole stinking with the blood and excrement of a host of terrified fowls. The place was crowded with African servants, and the racket of their chatter competed with the screeches and squawks of the chickens to create an unholy uproar. The floor was slippery, the stench was overwhelming; no matter how hard I tried not to breathe through my nose, I could not block out the dreadful odor.

Sol presided grandly over this scene of carnage. Draped in a long white apron decorated with dried gore, he grasped each hen by the legs and severed its throat with one swift slash of his razor-edged blade. As the decapitated bird's red juice spurted into a pail at his boots and slopped over onto the cement floor, he chanted, "Why did the chicken cross the road? To meet up with me!" In such moments his grizzled, sunken cheeks and his wild grin recalled the Joker, the villain in the early Batman comics.

Whenever Sout and I entered the shed, Sol gaily summoned us to the head of the line. "Boots! *Mishpocheh!*" he'd shout joyfully, favoring family over the several other boys who, like me, had been sent to supervise the servants. He snatched away the hen I carried in my arms and hefted it upside down, judging its weight of blood. He particularly relished this act because he knew that the poor fowl was something of a pet to me—I tended the chickens we raised from chicks in our backyard pen—and that inspired him to an extra dash of glee as he cut its throat.

If the hen laughed, I was too dismayed hear it. I had to watch while the last drop was drained from the convulsed carcass. Kosher law, as Sol never tired of reminding me, demanded that all the meat be bloodless. When at last I staggered from the shed, my throat was choked with suppressed puke. But Sout was unperturbed. "It's kosher, baas," he'd say serenely, hoisting the headless birds.

Sol was not only the town's shokhet, but also its principal *mohel*, or male circumciser. It was he who had slit my baby foreskin to honor Abraham's covenant with Jehovah, and every time I saw him, in the shed or at family get-togethers, my scrotum clenched. He used a different knife for circumcisions, of course, but in my nightmares I fancied he was cutting my tiny penis with his heavy shokhet's blade, before tossing my prepuce into his slop pail, along with the chicken heads.

Like his older brother, my grandfather, Mathew, Uncle Sol had ended up in Africa after a series of misadventures. In the great wave of migration at the turn of the twentieth century, millions fled Europe's familiar homelands for a variety of far-flung destinations, often as alien as the moon in their provincial experience. My grandpa, for instance, never really understood how he'd come to settle in a remote corner of the so-called Dark Continent, but Sol seemed to know exactly where he was and why. "I'm in *sheissland*," he said, "because the Lord, *baruch Hashem*, thinks that I'm a turd—and he has to be right, isn't it so?" In a final twist, the Lord had seen fit to condemn him to a life of ritual butchery.

All in all, the community didn't quite know what to make of Uncle Sol. On the one hand he smelled of stale blood, despite the harsh carbolic soap he used to scrub his hands and arms, and his jokes were often off-color or just plain rude. He delighted in pricking pretensions, particularly the Jews' precarious status as "honorary whites" in a racist culture. "Jews are Asians," he declared bluntly. "If Israel is our Holy Land, we can't rightly claim to be Europeans." In their cultural confusion, he said, "The Yids hereabouts blunder around like farts in a pickle barrel."

On the other hand, Sol was a noted scholar, a role long appreciated by Jews. The local rabbi regularly consulted him on the interpretation of passages in the Torah for his Sabbath sermons. Sol had the Talmud and its multitudinous commentaries at his fingertips, plus the writings of major Jewish philosophers such as Maimonides, his favorite. "As RamBam [Maimonides] said, 'Only in the days of the Messiah will we know what the metaphors mean . . .'"

At the family Passover Seder, hosted by Grandpa, these opposite aspects of Sol's character collided. Learned disquisitions upon the meaning of exile for the Jews were interrupted by a barrage of sly anecdotes about family members, plus the odd questionable joke. One moment he was quoting Gershon Scholem—"'Jewish Messianism is in its origins and by its nature a theory of catastrophe.' That's to say, Jerusalem is far more inspiring for our people as an aspiration rather than a reality..."—and the next moment he'd sideslip into gossip about who was *shtupping* who in the community, within and without wedlock. He countered outraged protests with his ritual retort, "cashmere in *tochas*," a play on Yiddish *kush mir in tochas*, "kiss my ass"—a jibe against the genteel pretensions of "honorary whites." Veering between esteem and disgrace, Sol kept everyone off-balance.

Another of Sol's unsettling quirks was his rare fluency in Ndebele, the local African language. Most whites spoke to their servants in Fanagalo or "kitchen kaffir," a kind of pidgin baby talk that made every speaker sound infantile. My grandpa, for example, often jumbled English, pidgin, Afrikaans, and Yiddish in one sentence: "O put *lo manzi und voetsek der hund.*" Translation: Take the dog outside and give it some water. Announcing litigation involving a business rival, he declared, "I am bringing against him a suitcase." Sol, by contrast, favored polyglot curses, including Yiddish *mamzer* (bastard), Ndebele *masatanyoko* (motherfucker), and English *shit-brains*.

When whites heard Sol chatting to the Africans in their native tongue, they were uncomfortable, as if he were breaching some unwritten code of nonfraternization. "If you talk to your slaves as if they were people, they may soon stop being slaves," he said. He claimed that truly successful colonizations depended on the absolute destruction of the native culture, either literally as in North America, or figuratively as in South America. "In our area we haven't quite accomplished that—not for want of trying!" Sol said. "So Africa will soon shrug us off, kosher and unkosher whites together, like fleas on a dog."

My feelings about Sol began to change as I grew into my teens. Through the fog of my childish revulsion at his manner and his trade, I began to recognize a truly extraordinary personality, one who might open my eyes to the world beyond our remote corner. After my bar mitzvah, I began to hang around the shokhet shed, hoping Sol would have time to sit down and chat with me. Many afternoons I waited by the door to his small apartment behind the shed until he returned from *Mincha*, the afternoon prayer session at the synagogue. He'd soon appear, carrying his worn blue velvet bag containing his yellowing prayer shawl and much-thumbed Torah that looked as if they had been handed down through the ages.

At first I was anxious about violating his fierce privacy, but he put me at ease with a cheery, "Shalom, Nephew! Welcome to my palace." His welcome was a momentous privilege for, so far as I knew, I was the only family member ever allowed into his *palace*, a marvelously shabby place submerged in a sea of books and papers, with islands cleared for his bed and desk. I imagined my mom's horror if she'd ever been allowed to view such splendid chaos; sight unseen, she pronounced it a pigsty. "I modeled my hovel on Karl Marx's study," Sol explained. "The man drowned in books. Fortunately, unlike him, I'm not plagued by boils on my bottom."

I'd sit on the unmade bed, the only place to perch, while he settled into the hard wooden chair at his desk a few feet away. To put me at ease, he removed his battered felt fedora, leaving his *kippah* to ride his springy salt-and-pepper brush like a small boat in wild waves. He usually stayed very still for a long moment while a gentle silence cloaked us both, calming my habitual fidgetiness. Then he'd begin to speak in a soft, almost caressing deep basso—the rough murmur of an aerial spirit swooping over oceans of wit and learning. He roamed from Abraham of Ur to Karl Marx, "from the ancestral father to the modern renegade son," a span of close to six millennia, practically the entire history of civilization. Sol claimed that at the end of his life, Marx, grandson of a revered rabbi, had returned to his ancestral faith, an act confirmed by shaving off his iconic beard. "As the proverb says, 'Better a Jew without a beard than a beard without a Jew.'"

As I listened, the thirsty sponge of my mind soaked up every syllable of Sol's talk. His wide knowledge and rich experience were a revelation to me, just as I was beginning to challenge the narrow local attitudes and assumptions of my colonial homeland. Day by day my soggy brain seemed to literally swell within the carapace of my skull. Sure, I didn't really grasp a fraction of his wisdom, but the amazing sweep and generosity of his intellect excited me beyond imagining. What a world out there awaited my discovery! So much to know; so much to do and feel and think...

After a session with Sol, my head buzzed so much I found it hard to sleep. "That man is making you *meshugah*," my mother grumbled. "I want to be crazy," I retorted. "Crazy's the only way to be!"

Though I was fourteen when these sessions began, and he was in his seventies, Sol always treated me as an equal, man-to-man. As a mark of our newfound closeness, he stopped calling me "Boots." In effect, he became my best friend, and I think I was his sole comrade, his only truly devoted ear.

As my love and admiration for him grew, I puzzled endlessly over the seeming contradictions in my granduncle's character. How could a man be simultaneously so intellectually refined and so thoroughly vulgar? Slowly it dawned on me that his high intelligence and his low wit were sides of the same coin. "*Hashem* boasts, 'Heads I win, tails you lose,'" he said, implying that for us the Creator's cosmos presents a rigged toss of the penny—an everlastingly confounding metaphor only the tardy Messiah could ever explain.

One of the oddest quirks in Sol's character was his passion for shooting game, rare for a Jew of his generation and origin. However, he told me that, as a boy, he'd hunted pheasants, ducks, and wild hares in the Ukrainian countryside with his father "to supplement the family pot." Back then, he said, his only gun was an ancient shotgun dating back to the Crimean War. "If you weren't careful, the *ferkakte* thing could blow your face off." Now he favored a bolt-action British Army Lee Enfield rifle, "the most reliable point-three-o-three ever manufactured," suitable for bringing down large antelopes such as kudu, his favorite target. Also, the gun was "handy to stop a leopard or a charging lion."

Since Sol preferred to hunt at night, we'd set out at dusk in his old Chevy saloon with its battered body and several missing floorboards. The rattletrap's flickering headlights cut a narrow tunnel along the strip of road whizzing by just under my shoes. Deep in the bush we made camp under a blaze of stars surrounding the Southern Cross—in Sol's graphic phrase, "a crucifix awaiting the Redeemer." Around midnight we fastened hunting lamps to our foreheads, he hefted his rifle, and we plunged into the silvered shadows of the luminous dark, following our twin beams.

Every so often Sol, leading the way, halted in his tracks and cocked an ear. "Listen, listen," he hissed, and I tried to mimic the intensity of his attention. Sometimes we heard a leopard cough or the brush of an owl's wings followed by a small scream as it nailed its prey. Then, suddenly, a pair of bright eyes might appear, transfixed by our headlamps. Judging its height off the ground, Sol reckoned it was some kind of antelope, perhaps a favored kudu. Leveling his rifle, he took careful aim.

The gun exploded—a crash of thunder and lightning in all that darkness. The recoil staggered Sol, and it was a moment before he could ascertain whether the bullet had hit home. Most times it hadn't; but when it had, we rushed to the spot to find the dying beast. More in sorrow than in triumph, Sol put another bullet into its skull to end its agony. Sometimes he allowed me to take a shot at a buck, but the heavy gun's painful kick threw me off, and I never bagged anything but a bruised shoulder.

On the trek back to our camp, Sol would revert to his jokey persona. If we glimpsed a pack of scavenging hyenas, he'd repeat the corny quip: "A hyena only copulates once a year, so why the hell is it laughing?" Somehow his patter made the African night less strange, and I snuggled in my sleeping bag beside the banked fire, listening to Sol ruminating about one thing or another, such as the belief that in southern Africa early human beings appeared many thousands of years ago, way before they colonized Europe. "If we open our ears all the way, we may hear an echo of those folk, who first began to wonder about their fate under the heavens…" Soothed by his hypnotic murmur, my drowsy mind slipped away into the deep silence of the dark.

In the morning, if we'd made a kill, Sol stopped off at a nearby kraal to tell the Africans where the carcass lay so they could retrieve it for themselves. "They need the protein more than we do," he explained. The deal was that the villagers provided him with a portion of sun-dried *biltong* (jerky), a treat we both enjoyed.

On the ride home Sol invariably exclaimed, "So, *chaver*, do you still wonder I could die laughing?" His high-hearted gaiety resonated with many undertones: his delight in the wild glory of the bush and the thrill of the hunt, muted by the darker shades of the slaughter we had shared, along with the sardonic irony of his accidental exile in *sheissland*, an epithet he reserved for colonial Rhodesia rather than the Africa he revered. In those moments, I came close to crying out that I sympathized in my own callow way, that I loved him more than I could say, but I was too shy. Anyway, his fond scowl as he squinted at the road seemed to say, "I know, my friend, I know."

When I finished school and was about to leave for university in Cape Town, a long way away, Sol invited me for one last visit to his place. As usual, we sat in silence for a while, but this time Sol did not ease into a monologue. Rather, he let the quiet run on for many minutes, as if there were no words to express what we both felt about the separation. He was a vital part of my life, and I could hardly imagine a world without his close presence; in truth, it was a little scary. How would I survive "out there" without his constant reminder to "listen, listen"? At the last moment, a dreadful thought popped into my mind: Would he actually slit his own throat someday and "die laughing"? Or would it remain a mocking metaphor? I wanted to ask him, but my tongue didn't dare form the question.

As it happened, Sol did slit his throat. He was diagnosed with a spreading Stage IV prostate cancer, and in those days it was untreatable. Rather than suffer the agonies of a slow demise, he lay down on the floor of his shed and, in my mom's blunt summation, "he did to himself what he'd done to a million chickens"—a kind of kosher quietus. If I listened intently, as he'd trained me to do, I imagined I could hear the echo of his laughter at "the biggest joke of all, my life."

THE BELLE OF PITTSBURGH

— *Barbara Graham* —

"You don't have to get all gussied up," I told her. "He's a *hospice* rabbi. He's used to seeing people in their bathrobes."

"I'm not people," my mother said, propped up on the hospital bed that had recently replaced the single bed in her apartment at the retirement place. "And I don't parade around in a bathrobe when company comes." Even now, at ninety-five, impossibly frail and tethered to an oxygen tank, Irene looked glamorous in her blue silk nightie with the ivory lace trim.

"He's not company," I protested halfheartedly, though, really, there was no point in arguing. My mother, the former belle of Pittsburgh, would die before she let any man see her in bedclothes without her "face" on.

Which is exactly what would happen, but we didn't know that yet.

Two weeks earlier, before the buildup of fluid in her lungs started squeezing the breath out of her, Irene called me on the phone sounding frantic. Hearing the wheezy panic in her voice, I panicked, too. Could this possibly be *it*? I wondered. After years of serial near-death experiences, had my mother—

the woman who joked that she was too mean to die—entered her final days, possibly her final hours? Could she be on the brink of disproving her point?

The answer was no. Maybe Irene had been telling the truth when she claimed that she was too mean to die. Maybe, like fictional characters bitten by vampires, she belonged to the ranks of the Undead. Maybe *she* was a vampire and, as her daughter, I, too, would be granted eternal life.

"Barb, help me, please," she implored over the phone. "I'm absolutely going out of my mind. You've got to tell me, the bronze silk or the leopard chiffon?"

It so happened that the retirement home was holding its annual black-tie ball that night, and Irene was in knots over what to wear. Forget that she was wobbly on her feet, even with the walker. Forget that she had lung cancer. The lady was a coquette—adored by men, envied by women—a flirty knockout with a smart mouth. And she had her reputation to uphold. She often boasted that when she walked into the dining room in the evenings, all heads turned in her direction.

"Every night they can't wait to see what I'm wearing. You wouldn't believe what some of them show up in," she'd scoff. *"Gym suits!"*

I counseled the leopard chiffon.

As happens so often, the thing you worry about most isn't what nails you. Irene's cancer diagnosis seemed to come out of nowhere two years before. She'd been admitted to the hospital for chronic, unremitting back pain when a routine chest x-ray (standard procedure in hospital admissions) revealed a few suspicious spots on her right lung. The biopsy confirmed adenocarcinoma. Lung cancer.

My mother chose not to treat the disease—or think about it. The tumors were small, and she didn't have a cough or any other symptoms. "I'm going to put it right out of my mind," she announced, taking the Scarlett O'Hara approach. "Then it won't bother me."

Other family members—doctors—were less optimistic. "Chances are, she won't make it to ninety-four," her first cousin, a Boston internist, told me privately. This man, along with a gastroenterologist nephew from Pittsburgh, was devoted to Irene and had been making pilgrimages to her "deathbed" for years. They came rushing to her side after the emergency colostomy, the bleed on her brain, the hip fracture—and always left astonished by her ability to bounce back.

"I'm afraid this time it's for real," Jerry, the Boston cousin, predicted sadly.

"She doesn't have long," Ken, the Pittsburgh nephew, agreed.

They should have known better. This was my mother they were talking about.

A CT scan taken six months after the initial diagnosis revealed no change in the size of the tumors. Another scan taken six months after that was even more striking.

"I've never seen this before, and I'll be damned if I can explain it," the oncologist said. "The tumors appear to be *shrinking.*"

I was stunned. The doctor was stunned. Boston and Pittsburgh were stunned. Irene seemed relieved, but not as surprised as the rest of us.

I took her to a deli to celebrate. She wanted tongue.

The deli lady held up the sliced meat for Irene's approval. My mother wagged her impeccably polished fingernail at the woman and rejected the meat.

"But I did just like you asked," the deli lady said. "I sliced from the tip."

"I said *near* the tip, but not the tip. The middle is too fatty and the tip is too dry."

At which point the deli lady heaved the whole fleshy V-shaped organ onto the counter. You could see the taste buds, the narrow groove down the center. "You show me where exactly," she pleaded, looking close to tears.

"There," Irene pointed with her scarlet talon. *"Near the tip, but not the tip."*

Sometimes my mother really did seem too mean to die.

Most people, except for certain family members and service professionals trying to please her, found Irene charming.

It wasn't her fault, really, that I was impervious to her charms. Or that she, for most of my life, seemed disappointed in me. We were so different, both products of our times, as well as our singular quirks and talents. I often felt as though we were mismatched, like two landmasses that don't fit together—say, Greenland and New Jersey. Irene longed for a daughter who would be just like her: a princess to her glamour queen, a stylish girl who prized glittering surfaces, powerful men, and a good address. But I was an arty, waifish girl who rejected the whole package. I shacked up with a stoned cowboy in hippie outposts from Boulder to British Columbia. When my man and I stayed in one place (with electricity) long enough to have a phone, I kept the number unlisted so she couldn't call me and tell me I was ruining my life.

That was in my twenties. By my mid-thirties, I'd dumped the cowboy, relocated from the woods to San Francisco with my young son, was earning a living (more or less) by my pen, and had married Hugh, a man my mother approved of—grudgingly—but later grew to adore. My parents were living in Florida then, so we saw each other infrequently, mostly on state occasions: big birthdays and anniversaries, plus the annual visit. Always, within a day or two, Irene and I would start to drive each other crazy, so I deliberately kept those visits brief.

I never dreamed I would become my mother's caretaker.

My mother never dreamed she would need a caretaker. Or that my father would die and leave her to fend for herself—or worse, leave *me* to fend for her. She never dreamed she would suffer agonizing physical pain or a bleed on the brain or a broken hip. And cancer didn't figure into her plans any more than the improbability of her own death.

Taking care of a sick, aging parent is not a job you can train for. The training happens on the job, by the seat of your pants, and you are always one step behind, playing catch-up with the latest crisis. The only predictable thing about this job is its unpredictability. And, in my case, the stubborn resistance of the caretakee.

Irene hollered and called me a bully. She accused me of turning her into an invalid, stripping her of her independence. The body that had been her calling card was betraying her, and I was the safest target for her rage. She fought me over everything. The aides, the walker, the installation of grab bars in the shower, the little alarm button she promised to wear around her neck but left in the bathroom the night she fell and broke her hip. The clincher was the move—urged by social workers and family members—from Florida to the retirement place in Washington, DC, where I live now, so that Hugh and I could look after her. Soon after she arrived, my mother started addressing me as "Mother" in a tone so sarcastic she sounded like me dissing her when I was a teenager.

At first becoming Irene's caretaker seemed like a joke, one of those crazy karmic twists of fate I might have found amusing if the story hadn't been mine. Rebel daughter spends entire adult life trying to escape clutches of fiercely narcissistic mother—only to have said mother wind up in her clutches.

My friend, the author and psychologist Mary Pipher, once told me that it's human nature to love what—and who—we care for. I never doubted that I would be a dutiful daughter to Irene, but I wasn't so sure I could let go of the defenses that had been hardening inside me since childhood like bad arteries. Compassion, yes, but love? I was determined to do everything possible to ease my mother's suffering, but could I unblock my heart?

I worried that I'd be an outlier, the rare exception to Mary's law of human nature.

My mother was a party animal and had been a celebrated hostess among her set in Pittsburgh, New York City, and Palm Beach. Although for years she'd been threatening supernatural retaliation if I dared to include her age in her obituary—*if she ever died*—I decided to throw a bash for her ninety-third birthday. She wasn't doing well (this was just a month before the cancer diagnosis), and I worried that she might not see ninety-four. But by the time ninety-four rolled around, her willfulness seemed to have driven the cancer, like defeated warriors, into retreat, so I decided to hold off on another party until the big ninety-five.

Plans were underway over Irene's protests—*I don't want a party, Barb!* which meant that she did—when the cancer finally caught up with her. Her right lung filled with fluid, and she was having trouble breathing. The pulmonologist wrote prescriptions for hospice and oxygen, and recommended draining the fluid from her lung so she would make it to the party. The procedure nearly killed her. Still, I refused to cancel. The caterer had been hired, and Irene's cousins and grandchildren—including my son, Clay—were flying in from around the country. Anyhow, this was *herself.* The smart money said she'd rally, and somehow, on the night of the party—one week after the procedure—the Belle of Pittsburgh showed up looking like a million bucks in the bronze silk.

I think Irene had the time of her life at that party. After the toasts, she confessed that she'd always been jealous of her own mother, envious of how much everyone who had known Bessie had adored her. If Irene had the looks, my grandmother—also a beauty—had the charisma.

"I finally know how my mother felt, and it's wonderful," Irene said, glowing, her paper-thin skin practically translucent. "Because tonight I feel that way, too."

It occurred to me that this might be the first time in her life that my mother felt worthy, good, deserving of love, just for herself—not for her appearance, her zip code, her fine antiques, the rich and famous people she met, the five-star hotels she stayed in, her Chanel suit, or any of the rest of it.

I'm pretty sure Irene knew that there would be no ninety-sixth birthday fête, and that the procedure that had siphoned off a liter of fluid from her lung was a temporary holding action. Still, she went right on as before: getting her hair done, complaining about the food at the retirement home, barking at the help for multiple offenses, agonizing over what to wear to the annual gala. For once, she took my advice and went with the leopard chiffon. It was her favorite, the dress she'd worn to my son's wedding.

The real clue that Irene knew something was up came in the form of a card she gave me on Mother's Day. The front of the card pictured five children in old-fashioned bathing costumes, holding hands as they splashed in the ocean. Inside, in her rickety scrawl, she wrote: "Happy Mother's Day! I know why Clay has turned out to be such a wonderful person. You have been a great mother. I know this is true because you have been a good mother to me. On Mother's Day and every day. I thank you for your caring and helping me in every way. Thank you, dear Mother."

This was the first time that Irene had addressed me as "Mother" without a soupçon of sarcasm. It made me wonder if she'd been expressing gratitude (in her backhanded, wisecracking style) all those other times. Or if somewhere along the way, her tone had shifted, and I simply hadn't noticed.

Six weeks after the lung procedure, two days after I'd asked the nurse if they were going to kick my mother out of hospice because she was doing so well, the phone rang early one evening. It was Irene, sounding scared and short of breath. "Can you please come over and help me?" she said. "I can't stand up."

From that moment on everything happened so fast: round-the-clock aides I rehired the minute Irene fired them (which she did often), stepped-up visits by the hospice team, delivery of the hospital bed and bedside commode, an emergency call to the fire department to bring oxygen the day the power failed because my mother had rejected the standard backup tank as too ugly to cross the threshold of her apartment, the start of morphine. Irene hated it all, except for the sudden, saintly appearance of Boston Jerry and Pittsburgh Ken at her bedside.

We all knew this crisis was no false alarm. This time there would be no astonishing resurrection. Yet, we were like dazed revelers on the *Titanic.* It was hard to believe that my mother's long-running exemption from the immutable laws that govern life and death was about to expire.

A few days into the final phase, which lasted two weeks, Gary, the hospice rabbi, came to call. He'd met with Irene several times before, and she'd grown to trust him and rely on him to help soothe her restless, fearful mind. (Plus, Gary was youngish, handsome, *and* Jewish! She liked flirting with him, too.) That afternoon I sat in with the two of them for the first time. No one had to say the D-word aloud for us to know what we were talking about. My mother said she missed my brother, who hadn't visited her in almost two years, and made me promise to stay in touch with him. When Gary asked her what it was about me that she was most proud of, she paused. "Who she is," she said finally. "Just. Who. She. Is." That may have been the first time in my life—certainly, in my adult life—when I felt truly seen by my mother.

A dear friend of mine once wrote, "You learn the world from your mother's face." That day I learned my goodness from my mother's face—even though her sight was failing and she could hardly see me. I told her I loved her and that I would miss her. This time there was no holding back, no going through the motions, no saying "I love you" with half a heart.

I think this is what Mary was talking about when she talked about loving the ones we care for.

Each day, a little more of my mother disappeared. First her sight, then her hearing. Her appetite was already shot. She started reaching into space for things that weren't there, and one afternoon she fell into my arms, weeping.

"I can't see. I can't hear. This is no way to live," she sobbed, as I held her and tried to comfort her—as if in that moment she really was my child and I was her mother.

Except, in point of fact, she was still *my* mother. Still Irene. Still the Belle of Pittsburgh. Not ten minutes after her outburst, she was fretting over what to wear the following morning when Rabbi Gary was due for his next visit.

"He's a *hospice* rabbi," I told her again. "He's used to seeing people in their bathrobes. You don't need to worry about putting on makeup or getting dressed."

But as long as she had a shred of consciousness left, my mother could not let herself go. What's more, I think she secretly believed that if she had the wherewithal to pull herself together she would be able to, if not outfox (in her case, out*dress*) death, at least delay it.

And so the next morning, instead of greeting Rabbi Gary in her favorite animal print dressing gown, Irene insisted on getting dressed. She couldn't stand or walk on her own, so Dawn—her Jamaican voodoo angel aide—practically carried her to the bathroom to put on her face. Then, somehow, Dawn managed to get her into her bra and the green-and-white striped blouse she'd chosen to wear for the occasion before her energy simply gave out. She toppled over into the easy chair by the hospital bed, her mouth slack, eyes shut, softly snoring. Dawn covered her lower half with a blanket since she'd collapsed before Dawn could get her into her pants.

I knew how much she wanted to see Gary again, so I tried to rouse her. So did Hugh and Dawn, with no success. When Gary arrived, he talked to her for a while, then said a blessing, but she didn't respond to him either. My mother seemed to be sleeping a sleep that was deeper than what we do in the night, but this side of death. Eventually, when it became clear that she'd slipped into unconsciousness, Hugh, together with Dawn and Gary, lifted her onto the hospital bed. She never awoke again.

In a way, her retreat could not have been more perfect,

more Irene. My mother used up every last atom of her awe-inspiring, superhuman energy reserves to make herself look pretty for the rabbi.

As Hugh and I kept vigil at her bedside over the next week, I realized that it didn't matter anymore what we called each other. Mother or daughter, those roles were done. Finished.

She was just Irene, a woman being swept away by the current that sooner or later takes us all. This was her story, her passage, and I was her witness. It was the first time I really saw her as a separate person—not in relation to me—and, somehow, during the hours I spent by her side not trying to do anything except be present, something came unhooked. All the things we fought over—my ripped jeans and wild hair, her ridiculous pretensions, my bad boyfriends and so-called irresponsible ways, her yearning for a daughter who would reflect her back to herself, my longing for a mother who would see me as I really am—seemed as insubstantial as a wisp of smoke.

Gone.

I buried her in the leopard chiffon.

BURIAL GROUND

—— *Richard McKenzie* ——

"We're lost."

Aza was speaking to me from a pay phone in a coffee shop in Sylmar, California, on July 27, 1972.

Nine days earlier, she had spoken to me from a pay phone in the waiting room of Roosevelt Hospital in New York City. "Mom died. Genie can't leave Vancouver; the orchestra has a concert. I'll bury her Thursday. The arrangements have been taken care of by the union. I'll be at home." Our apartment was practically around the corner from the hospital.

My mother-in-law, Rose Millenky, was a milliner, a member of the garment workers' union, retired, and living in the International Ladies' Garment Workers' Union apartments on Eighth Avenue. In a younger time, she was an adventurer, swimming across the Hudson River, hitchhiking around the country, climbing in the Adirondacks; if there had been sky-diving, she would have been right there. She was hardly a flit, though. She was intelligent, educated, and artistic.

When David Burliuk, already a major painter and poet in Russia, came to the Lower East Side, he and his wife lived in Rose's apartment building. She recognized the importance of his work and started hawking his paintings to family, acquaintances, galleries, passersby on street corners, and anybody else who would look to help get him established. His day job was writing for the Russian language newspaper. Rose's recompense was that he would write a review of Aza's dance recital. It was glowing. They became lifelong friends. Aza still has a bunch of his paintings to take care of us in our old age.

Rose had two girls. Aza, fathered by Samuel Cefkin (Pop), became a Martha Graham modern dancer, Broadway dancer, Broadway actor, and Actor's Studio early member. She picked me up after our first rehearsal playing my wife in a Tennessee Williams play, *A Period of Adjustment*, in Richmond, Virginia, and has kept me around for forty-eight years so far. She's an inveterate reader of history, politics, and periodicals from the *New Yorker* to the *Nation*, with fiction thrown in. Her sister Eugenia, known as Genie, was fathered by Abe Millenky. Genie was a violin prodigy, won a scholarship to Juilliard, hankered for a French horn player, switched to English horn and oboe so she could sit closer to him in the orchestra, and had her scholarship renewed in a few months. They married, shipped out to the Vancouver Symphony (British Columbia), and became union leaders in the orchestra—left-wing troublemakers.

In the last few years of her life, Rose slipped into presenile dementia. Aza came across her on the street in their old neighborhood, looking for their old apartment, lost, and took her home. We started watching her more carefully. One night we found her cowering in the stairwell of her apartment house, having had a nightmare. She had to save the children, the pogrom, the soldiers were coming. She had run from the apartment, locking herself out. We found her by chance when we punched the wrong floor on the elevator and were walking down to her level. Alzheimer's was upon her. Aza quickly made arrangements at a retirement and nursing home on West End Avenue.

Rose never lost flirting. When we picked her up for a drive through Central Park in our 1951 Riley Drophead, she would get in, give me her best come-on look, and murmur, "Hiya, handsome." Her eyesight, not so good.

A long-neglected breast cancer finally put her in the hospital, and then she died.

Aza hung out in the City for a couple of days, grieved, saw a few friends, and then flew back to Minneapolis, where I was on temporary duty at the Tyrone Guthrie Theatre. I'd been hired for the season, playing George in *Of Mice and Men*, directed by Len Cariou, and The Wall in *A Midsummer Night's Dream*, with Roberta Maxwell and Frank Langella, directed by John Hirsch, a truly brilliant director, in repertory.

John was another refugee, born in Hungary and spirited away in the late 1930s, before he could be swept up and sent to a concentration camp. His early memories were of winter, walking between rows of frozen bodies stacked like cordwood. When he was taken to safety, he was asked where he wanted to live. He looked at a map of North America and put his finger on Winnipeg, a dot on the landscape, where he became a major force in theater. In 1989, he died in his personal death camp, AIDS.

The Guthrie, a theater where many rising actors dreamed of spending time, for a season, or for a great part, housed a small, permanent group of experienced performers, not retired, just not interested in the daily tilting at windmills in New York and Los Angeles; the appointments, the auditions, the rejections, the bad scripts and plays. It certainly ain't all pretty. They could live in a beautiful city, work in a beautiful theater, do beautiful plays, ably directed, in front of the most intelligent and appreciative audience anywhere, and make a decent living.

The group included Robert Pastene, probably the best actor I ever knew or saw. Everything he did on stage, just walking through an entrance, was effortless. He understood the magic of acting, the ability to leave his personal demons in the dressing room and bring onstage only the demons of the character he was playing, though sometimes closely aligned. And Pastene had demons, demons that presented as severe physical stress, a frozen shoulder and stiff neck, giving him a look of imperious, total command on stage. He didn't need the look; he was in command. When he was Buck Rogers, on live television in New York, Aza played an enemy, Ishtar, goddess of something or other, who could look into her basin of predicting fluid and see all sorts of mayhem for which she would be responsible.

When Robert had finished a lengthy, successful run on a television afternoon serial and was visiting the Barter Theatre (a summer theater in the hills of southwest Virginia, where a lot of us began our lives in the business), he was having lunch in the soda fountain section of the local drugstore. There was a commotion at the cash register in the front of the store, and someone yelled, "Call the police. There's a killer in here, a murderer!" That was followed by the looming presence of a large, farmer-type man in bib overalls saying, "I'll hold him. Call the sheriff!" Bob looked around the drugstore for someone who would do such a thing, and then "Bib Overalls" pounced on him. It took a lot of talking and restraining to convince the man to let him up. It was true TV, Pastene *had* killed his wife—on *The Edge of Night*. (Now, that is not necessarily a small-town happening; a similar thing happened to me on East 42nd Street in New York, and again in the parking lot of a supermarket in Cleveland, when I was acting in the soap opera *Love of Life*, playing a con-man killer. My mamaw, in Tampa, once declared, "I don't care if he *is* a murderer, he's my grandson!")

It was only days after burying her mother that Aza got the call from Los Angeles telling her that her father had died from a heart attack that morning. His wife, Aza's stepmother, said he died in the shower; he was a clean old man, beautiful and clean.

Pop was a printer, a Linotype operator who learned his craft after he came over from Russia to Rochester, a jumping-off point for many Jews fleeing czarist Russia, coming in by way of Quebec. He joined the union after his apprenticeship. In 1911, he was asked to help a young revolutionary gangster escape the police, after she had held up a government courier, stealing important documents. There was a harrowing run through Belarus to the Baltic Sea, using a sort of underground railroad, a steerage journey to Montreal, then on to Rochester, where an older brother, a plumber, had migrated with his family. The steerage part of the journey was obviously horrific because Samuel never spoke of it.

There was a time when Rose, her second husband Abe, and Aza were living in Russia. Abe Millenky, Aza's stepfather, was a mechanical engineer who had been sent by Ford Motor Company to Nizhny Novgorod to build an assembly plant. Rose took this opportunity to travel deep into Siberia, where she found her mother quite ill and brought her back to western Russia. The woman died shortly after the reunion. While Rose was away, Aza stayed in Moscow with her father, who had been asked by *The Daily Worker* to go to Russia to translate and teach Linotype operating for a sister newspaper.

While the family was in Russia, Hitler was coming to power. Travel routes were closing, and Stalin still didn't like the Jews. Abe and Rose, being under the auspices of Ford Motors, felt safe enough, but they didn't feel so sure about an incredibly beautiful young Aza. On a weekend Volga River outing, a soldier had threatened to carry their teenager off to the mountains on his horse—he was probably *not* kidding around.

Sensing the impending danger, Pop prepared an adventure that included retracing a route to the Baltic Sea. This time, he'd take his daughter, and the police weren't searching for him. They traveled by train to Riga. The ship was a regular ocean liner, accommodations were light-years from the terrible scow he had sailed on several decades earlier, hunkered in a filthy bilge. Pop's only concern was the crush Aza had on a very handsome young sailor and the sailor's attraction to her.

They returned to New York and The Coops, sans sailor, and Aza went back to high school a celebrity.

I had met Pop a few years before Aza knocked me over. I was a union printer, as in International Typographical, as in Linotype operator. Looking for acting work, I didn't have to worry about having to quit temp jobs, like waiting tables, then trying to find a job after the acting job. I could work around New York. There were still quite a few newspapers then—*Times, Tribune, News, Mirror, Post, Wall Street Journal, Morning Telegraph*—and I was able to substitute for regulars who couldn't make it out of the Blarney Stone or McSorley's, or were on vacation, or when a paper, like the *Times,* needed extra operators to produce ads for its huge classified section in the Sunday edition. If all else failed, there was the *Journal American,* a rag on South Street between Battery Park and Fulton Fish Market. You could get a beer and a fish sandwich wrapped in butcher paper for a buck and a quarter and eat lunch in the park.

Pop was a retiree, allowed to work a few days a month for extra income and hang out at the shop for a while. After the *Daily Worker*—where he had worked since it started printing in 1924—stopped publishing in 1958, he retired. Since he lived downtown on the East Side, it was easy enough to catch a bus to the Hearst paper and work his seven-day allotment. However, he was not much of a hanger-outer.

I remember catching on at the *Journal American,* and sitting at the machine next to him, being struck by the neatness of this old guy. Composing rooms of newspapers were not particularly clean places to work; a film of printer's ink was on every surface, including the keyboards of typesetting machines, and there was the graphite dust used for lubrication. Pop didn't use a paper towel to wipe the grime from his keyboard and surrounds; he had a cotton dish towel with a bit of a clean smell to it, and he used it a lot, it seemed. Like most of the tradesmen of his generation, he wore a white shirt and tie, only he didn't roll up his sleeves, didn't unbutton his collar, didn't tuck in his tie, and didn't wear an apron. Clean old man. Handsome. Reserved. Didn't have anything to say to me, just a nod.

I never worked with him again, didn't know his name, never saw him again until Aza introduced us in Los Angeles. I was startled. You sit beside a host of printers over the years, in shops around the country, with and without white shirts and ties, with and without aprons, and a chance, one-time meeting becomes indelible; also, he's now your father-in law. Even more startling was that he remembered me. He recalled seeing my name on the sign-in board and had decided he wouldn't speak if I sat next to him. With a last name like McKenzie, I was probably an anti-Semite.

After Pop got his union card in Rochester, he moved on down to New York City, to the Lower East Side, and then with Rose and Aza into The Coops in the Bronx. The complex had been built by the United Workers' Cooperative Colony to house secular Jews, mostly Communists, who had fled the czar's Cossacks in Russia and, later, Stalin's purge—Communists but anti-Stalinists. The conditions for survival, especially on the Lower East Side, were far worse than the shtetls of Poland and Russia, thus the formation of workers' cooperatives that bought property and built living quarters, activity centers, and shuls for immigrants, including Yiddish-speaking camps like Kinderland, in the Berkshires, where Aza spent many summers.

So we're back in Minneapolis, where Aza got the call one week from the day her mother died, telling her that Pop was dead. I drove her to the airport, and she was on a plane to Los Angeles by midafternoon, sobbing, shaken. She had had time to prepare for Rose's death, as her mother had been failing for a while, and had been in the hospital for several days. But Pop's sudden heart-attack death seemed almost unkind, inconsiderate, selfish. And Aza had to do it alone: there were no understudies at the Guthrie Theatre. There were no friends to meet her, to hold her, to put her up. Her stepmother didn't invite her to stay (she wasn't called "Mean One" for nothing).

Mean One was still angry at Pop for dying on her, in the shower where the water ran out onto the floor. Also, her son from her first marriage was staying with her, and she had always been mad at Aza for having somehow dissed him. Aza had called him a lazy mama's boy, which was the truth, not a diss. Also, the old woman was in failing health herself.

Most of the arrangements for Pop's burial were handled by Workmen's Circle. Plots had been bought years before in the Workmen's section, where Pop would be buried next to his brother. This was Sholom Memorial Park, part of, but below, Glen Haven Memorial Park. That was the rub.

There were three recruited drivers (grandchildren of Pop's

friends) and nine mourners. Pop's widow, Mean One, had fallen quite ill and was unable to attend. That left Aza, once again alone, to take charge. They gathered in the parking lot of a small mortuary in the Wilshire District. Pop, a devout atheist, wanted nothing to do with synagogues, none of that opiate for him. The mourners divided themselves up, climbed into the cars that constituted the processional, and headed out to the San Fernando Valley, to Sholom Memorial Park, faithfully following the hearse.

After a few cautionary stops and starts, they crossed into the Valley, but it became noticeable to Aza and her young driver that perhaps the hearse driver might be in a little over his head: whenever he came to a stoplight, he'd consult a map. Somewhere along the route—which led past several cemeteries, but none called Sholom—a traffic cop in the middle of an intersection pointed to a yellow sign that read "Accident Ahead" and motioned for them to turn left. Away they went, now in real trouble.

Rather than follow the road, the hearse driver turned into a series of cul-de-sacs. The first one led to a neighborhood under construction, and the little roundabout was filled with stacked lumber, plywood, and cement bags. The street wasn't even paved. They managed to bump their way out, the hearse followed by three cars, mostly filled with elderly mourners with bladder issues.

The next circle was inhabited—bicycles, wagons, bats, balls, gloves everywhere—the street deserted. Aza saw a curtain drawn back briefly, then dropped, just like in a Western. The young driver said to Aza, "What is it with this guy and cul-de-sacs?" The ancient mourners in the backseat had now nodded off.

The next side trip was inhabited by actual people. As the driver got out to talk to a woman watering the lawn, a rubber baseball hit the side of the hearse. The driver ducked just in time. While he was asking for directions, kids on their bikes snaked in and out between the vehicles, staring into the hearse's window at the casket. An adorable little girl sitting on the curb near Aza's window smiled at her and said, "Would you like to play dolls with me?" displaying her array. Aza said she almost got out of the car. The conversation with the watering lady was not fruitful.

When this "Lost Tribe of Israel" was passing the same coffee shop for at least the third time, an *alter cocker* in the backseat yelled, "I gotta go!" The driver blew his horn and turned in. All vehicles followed. The driver of the hearse headed for a phone booth in the parking lot. Inside, the old folks lined up according to the severity of squirming. The Men and Ladies signs were not in the equation: the old guys were told to squat. In the café, Danishes and crullers were wiped out, with coffee and sodas. There was a pay phone on the wall.

I was in our apartment in Minneapolis, having just returned from the airport to pick up my parents, who had come to visit from Tampa. When the phone rang and the operator told me it was Aza, I accepted the charges.

"We're lost. I mean lost. The hearse driver hasn't got a clue. I'll tell you about it when I get home, if we're ever found. The driver is waving at us. We've been waving at him for the last two hours; now *he's* waving. I'll see you tomorrow, probably Saturday. I love you, 'bye."

When they got outside, there was another funeral procession in the parking lot, engines running. The hearse driver had obviously flagged it down. There were a lot more than three cars with that hearse; they even had a police escort. Pop's group piled in and followed, driving into very familiar territory, turning onto a road they had been on before, four or five miles through a canyon they recognized, to a cemetery they had been at before, Glen Haven Memorial Park. Pop's driver had seen the sign and turned around to journey back through the canyon, on to other dead ends. There was a mortuary office right there. What a guy.

One of the motorcycle cops, hand up to stop them, got in front of the hearse, escorted them around a corner, perhaps a couple hundred feet, and turned right into Sholom Memorial Park and the Workmen's Circle section. The hearse driver slid Pop's casket onto an available gurney and split. Aza was sure there were many cul-de-sacs to be lost in before his day was through.

The three young drivers and the policeman put the casket onto the straps of the prepared gravesite—the service had been expected much earlier, so nobody was around. They lowered him. After a short goodbye, a lot of tears, and a few laughs about the day, Aza tossed in her handful of dirt; the gravestone and the pebbles on top would have to wait. She knelt there for a few moments and was quite certain she heard Pop say to his brother resting beside him, "Misha, have I got a story for you. Oh, boy, have I got a story."

VIRGO

— Starhawk —

In life, in death, my mother was a Virgo, which means she was so many things that I am not: neat, well-organized, meticulous, good with details. She delighted in filing things in their proper places. When she got sick with cancer and faced the possibility of her own death, one of her laments was "What's going to happen to my files?"

On her deathbed, as my brother and I sat with her, she insisted on getting out her Rolodex and going through it, telling Mark who to invite to her funeral. By the time they got to the *E's*, he couldn't take it any longer. "Mom," he said, "you're dying. You've got to let go."

But letting go was not my mother's strong point. She had the tenacity of a pit bull when she got hold of an issue, and a loud and furious bark. She yelled when she was angry, or irritated, or simply anxious. We were a yelling sort of family—yelling when we were mad and yelling when we were happy. When we were apart, she would occasionally yell by mail, typing a furious letter at 3 AM and trudging out to the mailbox to send it.

I'm not sure if it was a tragedy or a blessing that she did not live quite long enough to get on the Internet, which would have saved her the trek to the mailbox. Long before the days of personal computers, my mother loved to ferret out and pass on information she thought would be illuminating or persuasive. Her letters to me—the ones that weren't tirades—were always thick with newspaper clippings, snipped from the *L.A. Times,* which she read standing up every morning, with it spread out on top of the portable dishwasher in her narrow kitchen. Sometimes I'd open an envelope and find nothing but a stack of clippings. They ranged from little items she thought would catch my interest to third-hand admonitions—for example, studies of the psychological impact on children of being born from artificial insemination, which seemed to pop up in great numbers after I mentioned to her that I was thinking of going to a sperm bank in order to conceive a child.

Actually, I wasn't. I was trying to get her to stop nagging me. She desperately wanted a grandchild, and I, by my late thirties, desperately wanted to be a mother, but not a single mother, and I had no partner. Not that I wasn't looking—but there are things in life you can make happen with will and determination, and others, like love, that seem determined by some other fate. Mom didn't really want me to be a single mother either. Both of us knew how hard that fate had been for her. But that didn't stop her nagging, scheming, and occasionally taking action. Once, when I came down to visit, I found her in the process of composing a personal ad for me to be placed in the local Jewish newspaper. Out of curiosity, I asked her what it said.

"I've gotten as far as 'Divorced Jewish female, highly intelligent...'" she said.

I questioned whether *highly intelligent* was going to be a big selling point. (I have a clear memory of cuddling on the couch with her when I must have been seven years old, asking her why I didn't have any boyfriends. I believe we were watching the Miss America Pageant at the time. "Boys don't like girls who are smart," she said. "Boys like girls who are sweet.")

I reminded her of this advice and suggested that her ad was not strategic. "And did it occur to you that you ought to at least mention the part about being a Pagan?" I asked. Since I was a well-known author of books on the Goddess movement and earth-based spirituality, since I spent my life writing and speaking about these topics, creating rituals, training priestesses of the Goddess, traveling all over the world doing workshops and lectures and Witch camps on the above topics, somehow the cold, stark "divorced Jewish female" didn't seem to cover it.

Mom brushed the comment aside. For her, my career as author and Witch, although it had lasted by then for a good fifteen years, was never more than a phase I was going through, a slight digression on the path she was convinced would lead me ultimately to becoming a rabbi. Or failing that, a psychotherapist, like her.

Her desire for me to be a rabbi was a bit odd, because my mother was not very religious. She had rebelled against her own Orthodox parents. We didn't keep kosher, went to synagogue only on High Holy Days, lit the Friday night candles only sporadically, and never kept Shabbos. She tended to dismiss the more observant members of the family—at least the younger ones—as hopelessly old-fashioned and to view the ultra-Orthodox as anal.

I don't know that my mother really believed in God—of any gender. For her, the mysteries were found in the depths of the human psyche. Why do we do what we do? What unconscious impulses move us? What hidden memories shape us?

When I was small, my mother seemed like a wise oracle who knew the underlying reasons for things. It was she who suggested that the boys who teased me and made me cry might actually like me. We'd snuggle in bed, and she'd tell me about her cases, about their childhood traumas that still hampered them as adults. Each was a fascinating mystery to be probed for clues that would explain their unhappiness.

Over time, my mother developed a near-religion of her own, a deep faith in the healing power of grief. Grief, she maintained, had its own process, its own timetable that could not be hurried or ignored. Grief is our healing response to loss, and if we let ourselves fully feel it and go through all of its stages, it will bring us through rage and despair, back to acceptance and restitution. She wrote a book about it (*A Time to Grieve*, by Dr. Bertha G. Simos) and became a sought-after expert in the field.

She came to her interest in bereavement out of her own terrible grief for my father, who died when I was five and my brother Mark was only nine months old. He was only forty-five at the time, but it was his third heart attack that carried him off. So death haunted my childhood.

There was nothing funny about my father's death. He had two older sisters who were albinos—perhaps a factor of their parents being cousins, a common practice among Eastern

European Jews of their generation. Not, as among royalty, to preserve some inheritance (they all barely scraped out a living either in America or back in the shtetls of what they always called Russia, but we now call Ukraine), but rather, I suspect, because they didn't get out much. My mother's parents were also cousins. When my grandmother Hannah came to this country at sixteen, she stayed with her Aunt Jennie in Duluth. Jennie's nephew Sam liked her, and when other boys came to call, he told them she wasn't home. So, they married, making myself and my brother as inbred as a pair of thoroughbred race horses, albeit not nearly so slim or fast on our feet.

My father's sisters suffered from bad eyesight and poor health, and Ida, the eldest, finally succumbed and died. They lived in Minneapolis, and we lived in Mishawaka, Indiana, where my father directed an institute for disturbed young people, a new post he held for just six months. I have only a few direct memories of him: how I loved the smell of cigarette smoke that clung to his clothing and how when he'd pick me up, my mother, knowing his heart was fragile, would get anxious. He was writing a book, completed shortly before he died, and I remember wanting his attention and being told, "Not now, Daddy's writing." It left me with the impression that writing a book was somehow a sacred activity, valued beyond all else, something to leave after you, like a child.

My father flew back to be with his mother after my aunt died, and my mother, baby brother, and I followed shortly after. I remember the plane ride—how the houses and cars below us looked like toys. Maybe I remember walking across the tarmac in my little blue coat, or maybe I just remember my mother, in years after, telling me how proud my father was of that little figure, how his eyes beamed at me.

That night, he had a heart attack and died. He and my mother were sleeping on the hide-a-bed in the living room; my brother and I were on the hide-a-bed in the dining room around the corner. We slept through it all—the cries, the ambulance.

In the morning, my mother came in and woke us. "During the night, Daddy got sick," she said and paused. My mother always had an irritating habit of pausing in the middle of her sentences, but this was somehow different. I knew, waiting in the bed, looking up at her, that something was deeply wrong. Something was about to be said that would change everything forever after. "And he died," she finished.

I remember little of the rest of that day—just hustle and bustle and tears. My aunt's funeral was scheduled, and all the relatives were on the way—most unaware that they would find two coffins, two to mourn for. My father's old friend Elmer took me and his daughters to the zoo—my mother in consultation with the rabbi decided the funeral might be too much for such a young child to witness. Wandering around the zoo, I felt as if an invisible gulf shut me away from those two girls. They had a father—I did not.

Loss changes us. Somehow in the night, I had become a different person, no longer a fortunate child, princess daughter of the king of our small world, but a figure of tragedy, The Girl Whose Father Died.

Ever after, my mother felt that she'd made a mistake in not letting me come to the funeral. I had a hard time grappling with the reality of my father's death—from my point of view, he had simply disappeared. Perhaps he was really still alive? Maybe he was a spy working a mission in Cold War Russia so secret he couldn't let anyone, even my mother, know. Unlikely, as my father and his brother constituted the Communist side of the family, but of course that was the secret that at five I was far too young to know. My mother didn't tell me until I was sixteen, a young antiwar activist going to demonstrations, arrested with Santa Claus for handing out balloons in Beverly Hills that read, "Peace on Earth: Stop the War in Vietnam!" She told me then how much fear they'd lived in during the McCarthy years, fear that someone would find out about my father's radical past (he'd disavowed the party during the Stalin purges) and that he would lose his job. She swore me to secrecy. I immediately ran out and told all of my friends, "This is so cool—my father was a Communist!"

My mother herself was not political—that is, she had political sentiments that were liberal and progressive, but she didn't act on them. She scarcely had time. Left at thirty-nine with two small children to raise on her own, she went back to work as a psychiatric social worker. We rented a small house in South Bend. I started first grade, where I was the smartest kid in the class, but soon learned not to flaunt it, but to act sweet instead. I was not so sweet at home, however. I resented the housekeepers who looked after us. I had lost my father—now I wanted my mother back.

But my mother was working, and grieving, and depressed. We had our moments of closeness, punctuated by more and more fights. By the middle of second grade, my mother decided she'd had enough of being a working mom. She packed us up and moved back to Duluth, where we lived in the flat above her parents and she could make do with my father's Social Security money. She wanted to be home with my brother, now age two, starting to talk and almost indecently cute. And I wanted a mother who would be home when I came home from school, with cookies hot from the oven like the mothers on TV.

I knew the other kids in our neighborhood were poor because there were six, eight, or ten of them in their families, and their houses had a distinctive, sharp acidic smell—the odor of poverty. The Catholics, on the other hand, had lots of kids because of their religion, but their houses didn't smell. I played with the kids in the neighborhood, but my mother got me a scholarship to a better school on the good side of town, run by the education department of the local university.

She drove me there and picked me up, which meant that she wasn't waiting for me when I got home, she was putting away the car. She wasn't the mother I had pictured in my mind, warm and cozy. But it wasn't really the warm cookies I missed; it was that something between us had ruptured with my father's death, and we never quite got it back. I wanted something I couldn't name or express and that she could no longer give me: I wanted her undivided, loving attention, I wanted my Dad back, I wanted to feel again that I was a fortunate child, surrounded by rock-constant, unassailable love.

I had dreams that my father came back and made everything all right. In the dream, he usually said that I could have a dog. I wanted a dog almost as much as I wanted a father, but my mother was not an animal person and didn't want another source of stress in her life. I didn't know it consciously then, but having had many dogs since then I recognize what they give us—exactly that rock-solid, unwavering, uncritical affection I so longed for and couldn't get from a Virgo, for whom nothing was ever exactly right.

After two years, Mom was dying of boredom in Duluth. We went out to visit her brother George, who had moved to L.A., and she found herself a job in California.

California! The very name implies the wonder of oranges growing in lush abundance in midwinter. Moving to L.A. from Duluth was like moving from the cold, frigid hell of the Scandinavians to paradise, albeit a smoggy one. My mother loved L.A., and her love for the place never wavered. When she got sick, she resisted my efforts to move her up to San Francisco, where I lived. "I hate the hills," she'd say. "They remind me of Duluth!"

My mother thrived in L.A. She worked as a therapist for many years for Jewish Family Services, then went back to school at age fifty and got her doctorate at the University of Southern California. She taught in their School of Social Work and then went into private practice, where she began making enough money to move us from lower middle class to solid middle class.

When I was fourteen, we bought a house in West L.A., and I finally got a dog, a puppy I named Jezebel. My mother's best friend Jeanne and her daughter Karen rented a smaller house on the same lot, and Karen also got a puppy. We bought them from a roadside stand, not knowing enough to realize it was a puppy mill and that both puppies were infected with distemper. I held Jezebel through the long, terrible day when she died, locked in the bond I'd longed for, her eyes fixed on me with a dumb trust I could not fulfill. I held the puppy as I did not get to hold my father, helplessly. We had other dogs later, but none was mine in the same way. One of my mother's clients gave her an older mutt named Mister, who had a bad habit of escaping and chasing cars. I spent a lot of evenings in the middle of the street crying, "Mister! Mister! Come home, Mister!" I don't know what the neighbors thought. After Mister chased a car that caught him instead, we got a dog from the pound named Argus who humped everything in sight, attacked mailmen, and barked furiously whenever I came home, usually long past the hour I was supposed to. If my mother were sleeping, he'd wake her. More often, she'd be lying awake, anxious, and working herself up to a new round of fury.

"Stop worrying about me!" I'd yell back at her. I was taking drugs and sleeping with strange men. From my point of view, those were not things to worry about. "I'm fine! Let go!"

Letting go, as I said, was not her strong point. Letting go is a spiritual good that goes with detachment and trust in a higher power. Her values were psychological. She believed in feeling her feelings and expressing them, at volume—not trying to release them.

I, however, was spiritual even as a child. The night my father died, I dreamed he came to me as an angel and told me not to worry, that he still loved me and he was all right. I asked to go to Hebrew school at an early age. My mother, though lacking faith in God, believed that religion was an important part of our identity. I think in her secret heart she also believed that if I grew up to be a nice Jewish girl, it would redeem her own rebellion, so she dutifully joined a temple and drove me to and from Hebrew school.

She was delighted that I had a bat mitzvah. As a child, she'd envied her brothers, who went to Hebrew school while she, as a girl, did not. They got bar mitzvahs, with all the attention and presents; she got nothing. Her parents took her out of her first year of college in order to enroll her thirteen-year-old brother in a yeshiva, a religious school that would ultimately prepare him to be a rabbi. It took her another decade to go back to school herself. She was filled with anger at the sexism with which she'd been raised—one more thing she never let go, but that I dismissed.

Oh, Mom, that's ancient history now. Get over it! I thought.

Years later, it was in part that same sexism that drove me into the arms of the Goddess. At the same time, Judaism began to open up to new roles for women. When I was invited to speak at a Jewish Feminist Conference in the late '80s, I decided to ask my mother to be my guest. I thought we might bond there, and it would be a way of tacitly saying, "You were right, Mom."

She was happy to be invited. But after she received the conference information, she called me in a fury.

"Do you know what they wrote about you?" she yelled on the phone, livid. My mother was fond of unanswerable rhetorical questions. Since I hadn't yet seen the schedule, I didn't know.

"For everyone else, it says, 'So-and-so is the director of Hillel, so-and-so has a PhD in this and that,' and you know what it says about you?"

"What, Mom?"

"It says, 'Starhawk is a nice Jewish girl who grew up to be a Witch!'"

I took a deep breath and practiced one of the calming and grounding techniques that I teach. "Mom," I admitted, "that was what I told them to say," and held the receiver away from my ear as she screeched into it.

"What? Don't you know that you have to list your credentials? How is anybody going to know who you are? You've written books, you have a degree—you have to list your credentials!"

We hung up in anger. I was mostly mad at myself for thinking I could invite her into my life and that we could recover some moment of that closeness I longed for.

But a few days later, she called me back.

"I talked to the rabbi," she said.

"Which rabbi?"

"Laura Geller." Rabbi Geller was one of the first women to become a rabbi, and she was an old friend of my mother. "We were driving down to a meeting, and I was telling her about my daughter, the Witch, and how I wished you'd become a rabbi like her, and finally I mentioned your name, and do you know what she did?"

"No, Mom, tell me."

"She pulled over, right there, and stopped the car. 'Bertha,' she said, 'are you trying to tell me that your daughter is Starhawk?'"

"'Yes,' I said, 'that's what I've been trying to tell you!' And do you know what she said?"

"I can't possibly imagine," I replied.

"She said, 'Bertha, let me give you a piece of advice. Leave your daughter alone! She's famous. She doesn't have to list her credentials—everyone at the conference already knows who she is. And besides, she's making a great contribution to Judaism doing just what she's doing.'"

Just as I was basking in this affirmation from Rabbi Geller (may her name be forever praised), my mother went on.

"And do you know how I felt?"

Proud, surprised, and relieved came to mind, but I knew enough to simply murmur, "No."

"I felt so hurt! I felt so left out! You're famous, and I didn't even know! You never told me!"

I wanted to say a number of things, like, "I don't feel famous" and "I think 'famous' is overstating the case—I'd say 'known in select circles.'" But I contented myself by saying simply, "Would you have believed me if I'd told you?"

My mother thought for a minute. "No," she admitted, "you're right. It had to come from the rabbinate."

Given the rabbinate seal of approval, I took my mother to the conference. We sat through the opening plenary, where a noted Jewish feminist scholar considered the question of how we, as feminists, can pray. Suddenly, she veered into an attack on the Goddess feminists whom, she said, lacked an ethical base. I sat there getting madder and madder, and my mother reinforced every verbal jab with a sharp poke in my ribs from her elbow.

Then the speaker ended her tirade by saying, "And, of course, in all of this I exempt Starhawk, whose commitment to social justice is well known."

That, of course, made me even madder. It was akin to being publicly called The One Woman Who Isn't Brainless or The One Jew Who Isn't a Dirty Money-Lender.

Finally, in the question period, I was called on. Fuming and sore in the ribs, I stood up.

"I'm Starhawk," I said, "and I want to respond..."

"Only questions," the moderator interrupted.

"Fine. My question is, How can a religion that's full of statements like 'Go into the land and kill the inhabitants thereof, spare not the women and children' claim to have a lock on ethics? There's a strong ethical framework in the Goddess traditions, and if I have a commitment to social justice, it comes just as much from being a Pagan as from being a Jew! I don't appreciate being singled out as The One Good Pagan!" Especially in front of my mother, I might have added.

I received a mild apology. But as my mother and I walked out to the car, she turned to me and said, "You know, those other women don't have the moral courage you have. I'm proud of you."

That was the one moment when I received from my mother everything I might have wanted. How I wish I'd said to her, "I am who I am because of you. I see your strength, your courage. I understand your struggles now in a way I couldn't as a child. I love you."

When my mother got sick a few years later, I pondered how to help her. Emotionally and practically, her needs were clear, but was there a way to help her spiritually? After she was diagnosed with lymphoma, I offered to do some healing work with her. She lay in the living room, and I led her into a light trance, planning to help her create a healing image upon which she might meditate.

"Take a deep breath, and think of a time when you felt good in your body, vibrant and healthy."

"I never felt good in my body," she muttered.

I stopped, feeling deeply sad. "How about when you were a child?" I asked.

"I felt fat. Big and fat. Big Bertha, like my name. I always hated my name."

"Well, did you ever have a fantasy about feeling good in your body?" I tried.

"Yes. I wanted to be a ballerina. Light and graceful."

"Can you picture that? Is there an image you can associate with it? A color?"

"White."

"Wonderful. Now, picture that white. What does it look like, feel like? What's its quality?"

"It's a dirty white. Like a used tutu."

I sighed. "We'll have to go with that."

She struggled with cancer for three years. Her cancer was sneaky, and it took years and many trials to confirm the first diagnosis of lymphoma. By then, it had spread. In all that time, she kept finding first one doctor, then another, who would finally be the one to truly take care of her in the way she'd always longed for. Inevitably, he would betray her—fail to answer a phone call or respond to a complaint—and she'd transfer to someone else.

Of course, what she truly wanted was for me to be the one to finally take care of her. I resisted. I had escaped L.A. in my early twenties, and I was reluctant to move back. Besides, every attempt I ever made to take care of her ended in some hailstorm of Virgoish rage at my imperfection, because I never could do things quite the way she wanted, never could offer her exactly what she needed most.

When I was nineteen, my mother had cataract surgery. In those days, it required a long stay in bed. I came home to take care of her. I cleaned the house. I washed the kitchen floor. She got out of bed, saw what I had done, and flew into a screaming tirade because I had used too much water. I walked out and refused to come back. My brother took over her care. Of course, now I understand that she wasn't really angry about the water; she was furious because she wanted something from me that I couldn't give her, just as I wanted something from her: the love so perfect it would bring the dead back to life.

In June 1992, she was well enough to come up to my wedding in San Francisco. Yes, I had finally found a partner, with no help from the personal ads, and while he wasn't Jewish, I pointed out to my mother that he was male and she'd better settle for that. In fact, when she met David, her comment was, "You've finally met a real man—I can die now!" Deconstructing that statement, I understood her to mean, perhaps unconsciously, that if I ever supplanted our mother-child bond with a partner bond, it would kill her. But I didn't share that thought.

Nonetheless, she proceeded to die. When I came back from our weeklong honeymoon, I rushed down to L.A. and was shocked to see how much she had deteriorated. But her doctors assured me they just needed to adjust her medication— that at the rate her tumor was growing she'd live another year, even if they did nothing. I began, however, to prepare mentally for a time when I would go down and take care of her, possibly at the end of the summer, during which I had a full travel schedule of workshops to give.

In August, however, my brother stopped by for an impromptu visit between music workshops, which he taught, and we got a call to come down immediately. "Your mother may not last the night," we were told, too late to get a plane that night. At the same time, my husband got a call that his father had had a serious stroke. My brother and I flew down on the first flight in the morning and found that Mom had rallied. She was awake, conscious and talking, Rolodex at the ready.

Mom faced her death with the same combination of courage and irritability with which she faced life. An intern came in to take a blood sample, and she batted him away.

"No," she said. "I'm tired of being stuck and hurt. Go away! I'm done with that."

"But we have to take your blood," he said. "We need to check your potassium level. If it gets out of balance, you could have a heart attack!"

"A heart attack!" she cried with glee. "That would be the best thing that could happen. I'm dying! Now go away."

His look of chagrin was the funniest part of the whole sad event. But after we ditched the Rolodex, the day took an upward turn. Mom's brother and her favorite niece came to say goodbye. Old friends and devoted students came to pay her tribute. In between visitors, I found myself possessed with a sort of panic. There were things she knew, information that she had that I would no longer have access to once she was gone. There were things about her that I might forget, if I didn't fix them in memory while I still had her there. I kept asking her questions. "What's your favorite color?" "What year was Daddy born?" There were things I still counted on her for, and I wasn't prepared yet to let her go. There was something I still needed from her and this was my last, my very last, chance to get it.

"Why are you asking me these things? Stop bothering me!" she snapped.

In the afternoon, her breathing became labored. As her lymph system stopped functioning, she was slowly drowning in her own fluid. I offered to do a little trance work with her, to make her more comfortable.

"You're floating in a dark pool," I murmured. "Deep beneath the earth, and you're a drop of water. Letting go. Dissolving into water. At peace, at home in the water..."

I'd led the guided journey often—starting as a drop in the heart of the mountains, rising up to become a bubbling spring, following the stream down to become a river, pouring out into the ocean, evaporating up into rain, falling down to soak into the ground and become again part of a deep pool under the earth. But as I began to suggest that she felt herself rising, she stopped me.

"No. I'm going in a different direction now."

At last, my mother was letting go.

Finally, her discomfort became so great that the doctors gave her morphine. She slipped into unconsciousness. Mark and I watched her throughout another long day. Mostly she slept, but every now and then she would awaken with a start and a labored gasp and sit up with a look of terrible panic. When she did this, we'd hold her hands, and I would lead her again into the dark pool, the comforting embrace of water. We'd said the *Shemah* with her—the Jewish prayer that one is supposed to say when dying—while she was still conscious. "Hear, O Israel, the Lord our God, the Lord is One." And so, after all, we were able to offer her some small measure of spiritual comfort.

At the very end, my brother held one hand, and I held the other. We tried to help her sit up, to ease her breathing, which had become not so much a death rattle but a horrible rasping as her lungs filled with fluid. And so she died, supported by both her children, who after all the nagging, and the fury, and the yelling nonetheless loved her dearly.

We sat with her for a little while. My brother put on some music he'd recently recorded. It was an Irish tune, and as its lively notes jigged around the room, I suddenly felt a great sense of relief and peace. It was as if a portal had opened to some sunny meadow where my mother could at last feel light and free, without pain, dancing joyously like a ballerina.

"What's that tune?" I asked Mark.

"I wrote it for a friend who lost his favorite pet," he said. "It's called 'Kicking Big Dog Upstairs.'"

Epilogue: My mother died just before her seventy-fifth birthday. I decided to celebrate it with a gathering in her honor, something she would have liked. She loved lively discussion with intellectual women. So I threw a women's party, a dessert potluck where we could tell our own stories of grief and loss. We gorged on cake and chocolate mousse and talked about death, life, and grief, achieving at last a perfect synthesis of the smart and the sweet.

Shortly after, I was seized with an inexplicable but intense need to clean out my office, go through my files and reorganize them, and order the books overflowing from my bookshelves. In the midst of the chaos, I got a call from my brother. "What are you up to?" I asked him.

"I don't know why," he said, "but suddenly I got in the mood to clear off the piles of paper from my desk. And then I had to reorganize my files."

"Me, too," I admitted.

A long pause, and then in unison we both cried out, "Mom!"

When I began this story, I thought there was humor in it. Now, I'm not so sure. My brother and I often laughed about Mom, but she never laughed about herself. We credited her with a very dry sense of humor, sure that she was saying some of the outrageous things she said to be funny. But now, I don't think so. Humor calls for a bit of distance, a perspective on who we are. My mother never stood back from her own life.

She was possessed by her emotions, and she believed in fully feeling every feeling from rage to grief to joy. I wish she could have had more of the latter and less pain. With all her anger and her irritating traits, she spent her life helping people and turning her own grief into healing for others. Surely she deserved more from life than to end it in such misery, never quite getting what she longed for, except perhaps at the very end.

But humor helped us. To laugh is to take a step out of the muck of emotion, to let the silt of resentment settle out and the streams of love run clear. Through the stifling hot days of an L.A. summer, we packed up her things, rented a U-Haul, and drove what I couldn't let go of back to San Francisco. For hours, my brother, who can remember jokes, told long, convoluted stories that generally began, "God and Moses were playing golf." As the miles rolled behind us, we laughed away the bitterness and the last dregs of disappointment, relinquishing all that we could never quite get and accepting the priceless gifts our mother did give us: her unflinching honesty, her courage, and her imperfect love.

The flight from Miami to Newark was creepy enough: my mother, in her coffin, was somewhere in the belly of the plane; my siblings and I, sitting in coach, told funny Mom stories, as if the last year of suffering through cancer treatments hadn't existed. We had all flown to West Palm Beach to be with Mom when she died—my sister and brother from New Jersey and Pennsylvania and me from Paris, where I was living then.

She had died while my brother and I shopped for sneakers at the mall. I had forgotten to pack shoes. In fact, luggage became the theme of that day. And creepy hardly begins to describe what happened next.

I remember not wanting to leave Mom after she died, even though I hated sitting with her body in that cold hospital room. My siblings and I said our silent goodbyes and headed to her condo to pack our clothes. We also needed to pack her clothes—that is, one last outfit for her to wear into the grave. We argued about that one: my sister preferred a blue suit my mother sometimes wore; I wanted her to dress for a party. My mother was a party girl.

I won the battle—as youngest and brattiest child, I usually won all battles. I picked out the dress, the bra, the panties, the jewelry, and the shoes (red heels!) and packed them in my suitcase, on top of my clothes. (Apparently I had forgotten more than sneakers and had plenty of room in my bag.) The funeral was set for the next day in Trenton, New Jersey, where we had all grown up.

I remember one other strange thing about that flight home: we laughed. We couldn't stop laughing. We had been crying for a year, since her diagnosis with ovarian cancer. Hours after her death, we stopped crying and instead howled with laughter. Remember how Mom used to knock every baseball out of the park? Remember the story about the bad date, when she climbed out of the bathroom window of the restaurant to escape the guy? Remember when we thought we had tricked her into thinking we were asleep in our beds, and she met us at the front door when we sneaked back in later that night?

The plane landed, and we headed to baggage claim. We were groggy with exhaustion and emotional overload. We stood numbly at the carousel, along with the hundreds of other passengers, waiting for the luggage to descend.

First, before any suitcase dropped through the chute, a single shoe rolled down and onto the revolving conveyor belt. A red high-heeled shoe. We stared at it, our mouths hanging open. There were murmurs and giggles from the crowd. Mom's shoe! I grabbed it and tucked it under my arm. And then a dress seemed to float down onto the carrousel, my mother's diaphanous flowered sheath. It even held a ghostly form for a moment before it crumpled onto the conveyor belt. I lunged for it and held it to my chest. There was a pause, a breathless moment, when the crowd watched and the unthinkable happened. My mother's bra descended. It was a large DD bra, lacy, lovely, and private! I grabbed it up and hid it in my arms. Stockings floated down next and then another red shoe, as if it were chasing the taupe legs down the chute.

The crowd was laughing by then. My siblings were murmuring to each other. I was hugging my mother's clothes for dear life.

Death is indecent! Death should be hidden!

Finally, my suitcase fell onto the conveyor belt. It was partially open, all the contents spilling out from a broken zipper.

It was a mess; I was a mess. It couldn't contain my mother's wardrobe; I couldn't contain my grief. I couldn't comprehend that she was really gone, yet here came proof that she was still around, still making herself known, one article of clothing at a time.

ACKNOWLEDGMENTS

My thanks to the twenty-three authors in this collection who loved, lost, laughed, and shared their stories.

At North Atlantic, I'm grateful to Jessy Moll, Roslyn Bullas, Anne Connolly, Kat Engh, and copyeditor Laura Shauger. A big thank you to everyone at Random House responsible for making sure this book appears on shelves worldwide.

As always, I count Jill Marsal of Marsal Lyon Literary Agency as one of my life's blessings. Her unflagging support—which includes not rolling her eyes when I run a really terrible anthology idea by her—gives me the confidence (and courage!) to keep going.

In the *last but not least* category, I give loving thanks to Alisa and Eugene Law, Matt and Erica Sosnick, and my beloved grandchildren: Olivia, Sophia, Lily, and Joshua.

ABOUT THE CONTRIBUTORS

Barbara Abercrombie teaches in the University of California, Los Angeles Extension Writers' Program and has published novels, nonfiction, and children's books, as well as essays, poetry, and articles in national publications. Her latest books are *Courage and Craft: Writing Your Life into Story* and *Cherished: 21 Writers on Animals They Have Loved and Lost*, and she writes a weekly blog. Her latest book is *A Year of Writing Dangerously*, published by New World Library. She lives with her husband in Santa Monica, California, and Twin Bridges, Montana. She can be reached at www.BarbaraAbercrombie.com.

Sam Barry is the author of *How to Play the Harmonica: And Other Life Lessons*, and coauthor (with his wife, Kathi Kamen Goldmark) of *Write That Book Already! The Tough Love You Need to Get Published Now*. Sam shares writing duties with Kathi in "The Author Enablers," their monthly column in *BookPage*. Sam tours with the all-author rock band the Rock Bottom Remainders and the San Francisco band Los Train Wreck. Visit Sam online at www.KathiandSam.net.

Joshua Braff graduated from New York University and received an MFA in creative writing and fiction from St. Mary's College of California. While a student, he published three short stories in national literary journals. Joshua is the author of the novels *The Unthinkable Thoughts of Jacob Green* and *Peep Show*. He is at work on his next book and lives in St. Petersburg. Visit him online at www.JoshuaBraff.com.

Zoe FitzGerald Carter is the author of *Imperfect Endings: A Daughter's Story of Love, Loss, and Letting Go*, a finalist for the National MS Society's Books for a Better Life Awards (Inspirational Memoir category), and a Barnes & Noble Discover Great New Writers pick. Zoe was born in Paris and is a graduate of Columbia Journalism School. She has written for the *New York Times, San Francisco Chronicle, Salon, Vogue,* and more. She is working on a novel and can be reached at www.ImperfectEndings.com.

Amy Ferris is an author, screenwriter, editor, feminist, wife, daughter, sister, and friend. Her memoir, *Marrying George Clooney: Confessions from a Midlife Crisis,* is being produced as an Off-Broadway play. Her essays have appeared in many anthologies, including *He Said What?* Amy's anthology, *Dancing at the Shame Prom,* was coedited with Hollye Dexter. She lives in Pennsylvania with her husband, Ken, and their two cats, Bella and Lotus.

Benita (Bonnie) Garvin is an award-winning film and television writer and producer. Her original film *The Killing Yard,* starring Alan Alda, premiered at the Toronto Film Festival and was nominated for a host of awards. Bonnie was nominated for an Edgar Award and won a special media award from the American Bar Association for the film. In addition to her many projects in the United States, Bonnie also has credits in European film and television. She is part of the faculty of the nation's most prestigious film school, the University of

Southern California, where she teaches screenwriting. Bonnie teaches screenwriting privately as well, and hosts weekend writing workshops around the country.

Sherry Glaser-Love is the author and performer of *Family Secrets,* Off-Broadway's longest running one-woman show. She received the L.A. Outer Critics Circle Award, South Florida's Carbonell Award for Best Actress, the NY Theater World Award for Best Debut, a nomination for a Drama Desk Award, and L.A.'s Ovation Award. Her autobiography is *Family Secrets: One Woman's Look at a Relatively Painful Subject.* Her newest stage works are *Oh My Goddess!* and *The Adventures of Super Activist Mother.* She is a founding member of the peace activist group Breasts Not Bombs.

Kathi Kamen Goldmark is the author of *And My Shoes Keep Walking Back to You,* a novel; coauthor of *The Great Rock & Roll Joke Book, Mid-Life Confidential: The Rock Bottom Remainders Tour America with Three Chords and an Attitude,* and *Write That Book Already! The Tough Love You Need to Get Published Now;* and has contributed essays to several anthologies. With her husband, Sam Barry, she coauthors "The Author Enablers" column in *BookPage.* Kathi is founder of the all-author rock band the Rock Bottom Remainders and "Don't Quit Your Day Job" Records, author liaison for high-profile literary events, and was a longtime producer of the radio show *West Coast Live.* A 2007 San Francisco Library Laureate and winner of the 2008 National Women's Book Association Award, she likes to think she is ready for anything. Visit Kathi online at www.KathiandSam.net.

Barbara Graham is an essayist, playwright, and author who has written for *Time; O, The Oprah Magazine; Glamour; More; National Geographic Traveler; Redbook; Utne Reader; Vogue;* and many other publications. She is the author of *Women Who Run with the Poodles* and editor of the best-selling anthology *Eye of My Heart: 27 Writers Reveal the Hidden Pleasures and Perils of Being a Grandmother.* Her plays have been produced Off-Broadway and at theaters around the United States.

Carrie Kabak is the author of *Cover the Butter,* a 2005 Independent Booksellers pick. She has received commendation as an illustrator by *Writer's Digest,* was named illustrator of the month by the Society of Children's Writers and Artists, and was a finalist for the Eric Hoffer (DaVinci Eye) Award for superior cover design. Her second novel, *Deviled Egg,* is in progress. Visit Carrie online at www.carriekabak.com.

Aviva Layton is the author of the novel *Nobody's Daughter* and several children's books. She has taught literature at universities, colleges, and art schools and has reviewed plays, books, and film for newspapers, journals, and radio arts programs in the United States and Canada. She has had essays published in two anthologies, *The Other Woman* and *The Face in the Mirror.* Born in Sydney, Australia, Aviva lived for many years in Montreal, Toronto, and London. She currently resides in Los Angeles, where she works as a literary editor. Aviva is married to author and architect Leon Whiteson.

Barbara Lodge's essays have appeared in the *Sun, Whole Life Times, Amarillo Bay, Clever Magazine,* and the upcoming anthology *It's All in Her Head.* An essay written under her pen name, Leigh Stuart, was published by Seal Press in the anthology *Dear John, I Love Jane,* which was a Lambda Literary Award finalist. She holds a BA in English and a Juris Doctor and lives in Los Angeles with her two teenage children.

Malachy McCourt is a Brooklyn-born, Limerick-reared author and raconteur who has been a longshoreman, radio personality, film and theater actor, playwright, and, in 2006, a Green Party gubernatorial candidate in New York. He is the author of *A Monk Swimming,* which earned best seller status in the United States and abroad; *Singing My Him Song; Bush Lies in State; Malachy McCourt's History of Ireland; The Claddagh Ring: Ireland's Cherished Symbol of Friendship, Loyalty, and Love; Harold Be Thy Name: Lighthearted Daily Reflections for People in Recovery;* and *Danny Boy: The Legend of the Beloved Irish Ballad.*

Richard McKenzie began to write after his Air Force service, at his father's newspaper in Blountville, Tennessee. This was interrupted by nearly five decades of acting. His theater work includes leading roles at Arena Stage, Washington, DC *(The Iceman Cometh),* Tyrone Guthrie Theatre, Minneapolis *(Of Mice and Men),* Westport Playhouse *(Uncle Vanya),* and Mark Taper Forum, Los Angeles *(Lost Highway).* Off-Broadway performances include *Nobody Hears a Broken Drum* and *A Whistle in the Dark,* and Broadway plays include leads in *That Championship Season, The National Health, Uncle Vanya,* and *Indians.* Film credits include *Doc, Being There, Some Kind of Hero, Man on a Swing, In Love and War,* and television work in *Roots, It Takes Two* (series regular), *All in the Family, Archie Bunker's Place, Love of Life* (daytime series, fifty to sixty episodes), and *In the Heat of the Night.*

Jacquelyn Mitchard's first novel, *The Deep End of the Ocean,* was named by *USA Today* as one of the ten most influential books of the past twenty-five years, second only to the Harry Potter series, and was the first novel Oprah Winfrey chose for her book club. The novel was transformed into a feature film produced by and starring Michelle Pfeiffer. Other novels include *The Most Wanted, A Theory of Relativity, Twelve Times Blessed, The Breakdown Lane,* and *Cage of Stars.* She has published five novels for young adults, including *Now You See Her, All We Know of Heaven, The Midnight Twins, Look Both Ways,* and *Watch for Me by Moonlight.* For mature young adults, she has written *The Things We Saw at Night* and *The Things We Saw in the Dark.* She is a contributing editor for the Disney parenting magazine *Wondertime,* and writes for *More, Parade,* and *Real Simple,* among other magazines.

Christine Kehl O'Hagan is the author of *Benediction at the Savoia,* a novel, and the memoir *The Book of Kehls.* Both books received starred Kirkus reviews, the latter a Kirkus Best Book of 2005 selection. Her essays have appeared in *Between Friends, The Day My Father Died, Lives through Literature, The Facts On File Companion to the American Novel, Exploring Literature, For Keeps, The Face in the Mirror,* and *He Said What?* She received the Jerry Lewis Writing Award and has contributed to the *New York Times, Newsday,* and several Long Island publications. O'Hagan lives on Long Island with her husband and is working on a second memoir.

Karen Quinn began writing in her mid-forties after she was laid off from a corporate job, started a Manhattan consultancy helping families get their children into the city's best schools, sold the business, and decided to try to write about it. Her first novel was the best seller *The Ivy Chronicles*. She has written four other books, including *Wife in the Fast Lane, Holly Would Dream, The Sister Diaries,* and *Testing for Kindergarten.* Movie rights were optioned for *The Ivy Chronicles* and *Holly Would Dream.* Karen recently developed a game called *IQ Fun Park* to help parents get their children reading for kindergarten testing. Karen also runs a website helping parents with admissions and school placement at www.TestingMom.com.

Dianne Rinehart has worked in Moscow, Ottawa, Toronto, and Vancouver as an editor, reporter, and columnist for some of the largest newspapers and magazines in Canada and the United States. She is a senior editor at the *Toronto Star.* Her work has appeared in the anthology *He Said What?* But her most important achievement to date is colaunching the organization Give Girls a Chance (www.givegirlsachance.org), to educate girls around the world. Their motto is: Educate a girl. Change the world.

Jenny Rough is a lawyer who switched jobs to launch a career as a freelance writer. She has written articles for the *Washington Post, Los Angeles Times, More, Whole Living, Yoga Journal, USA Weekend,*

AARP, and *Writer's Digest,* among other publications. Her work has also appeared as commentaries on public radio. She is currently working on a memoir about healing from infertility.

Starhawk is the author of twelve books on Goddess religion, earth-based spirituality, and activism, including *The Spiral Dance; The Earth Path;* her children's picture book, *The Last Wild Witch;* and her latest, *The Empowerment Manual: A Guide for Collaborative Groups.* She consulted on the Women in Spirituality series of documentaries for the National Film Board of Canada, and together with director Donna Read founded Belili Productions, making documentaries on issues concerning women and the earth. Their first, *Signs Out of Time,* explores the life and work of archaeologist Marija Gimbutas and was released in 2004. In November 2010 they released *Permaculture: The Growing Edge,* about the worldwide movement in regenerative ecological design. Her novel, *The Fifth Sacred Thing,* is in preproduction with Yerba Buena Films to become a feature-length movie. She works with the Reclaiming extended network of teachers and ritual makers. A committed activist for global justice and the environment, Starhawk also teaches Earth Activist Trainings: courses in permaculture and regenerative design with a focus on organizing and activism and a grounding in earth-based spirituality.

Ellen Sussman is the author of *French Lessons* and *On a Night Like This,* both *San Francisco Chronicle* best sellers. She is also the editor of two anthologies, *Dirty Words: A Literary Encyclopedia of Sex* and *Bad Girls: Twenty-six Writers Misbehave,* the latter of which was a *New York Times* Editors' Choice and a *San Francisco Chronicle* best seller. She has published numerous essays in anthologies, including *The Other Woman,* and a dozen of her short stories have appeared in literary and commercial magazines.

Michael Tucker is a veteran actor and recipient of three Emmy nominations and two Golden Globe nominations for his role on *L.A. Law.* His theater credits are extensive, including plays throughout the United States, such as *Moonchildren, Mother Courage, Trelawney of the Wells,* and *I'm Not Rappaport.* Film credits include *Radio Days, The Purple Rose of Cairo, An Unmarried Woman, The Eyes of Laura Mars, Network,* and more. His first book was *I Never Forget a Meal: An Indulgent Reminiscence,* part cookbook, part memoir; *Living in a Foreign Language: A Memoir of Food, Wine, and Love in Italy* was published in 2008 and is now available in paperback. He received the Good Guys Award from the National Women's Political Caucus for his work on women's health issues. His debut novel will be published next spring by The Overlook Press.

Leon Whiteson is a Southern Rhodesian–born (now Zimbabwe) architecture critic and writer. He is the author of *A Place Called Waco: A Survivor's Story; Dreams of a Weeping Woman; A Garden Story; A Terrible Beauty: The Positive Role of Violence in Culture, Life, and Society;* and an impressive collection of books and articles on architecture. He has an essay in the anthology *The Face in the Mirror.* Leon lived in England, Spain, Greece, and Canada before settling in Los Angeles. He is married to author Aviva Layton.

Victoria Zackheim (editor) is the author of the novel *The Bone Weaver* and editor of four anthologies: *The Other Woman: Twenty-one Wives, Lovers, and Others Talk Openly about Sex, Deception, Love, and Betrayal; For Keeps: Women Tell the Truth about Their Bodies, Growing Older, and Acceptance; The Face in the Mirror: Writers Reflect on Their Dreams of Youth and the Reality of Age;* and *He Said What? Women Write about Moments When Everything Changed.* Victoria adapted five essays from *The Other Woman* and created a play, produced by Jonathan and Hillary Reinis Productions. She is story developer and writer of the documentary film *Tracing Thalidomide: The Frances Kelsey Story* and writer for *Where Birds Never Sang: The Story of Ravensbrück and Sachsenhausen Concentration Camps,* both with On the Road Productions. Her screenplay about the Maidstone prison escape has been optioned by Identity Films. A 2010 San Francisco Library Laureate, she teaches personal essay writing in the University of California, Los Angeles Extension Writers' Program.